# MILITIAS IN THE NEW MILLENNIUM

*A Test of Smelser's Theory of Collective Behavior*

**Stan Weeber and Daniel G. Rodeheaver**

**University Press of America,® Inc.**
**Dallas · Lanham · Boulder · New York · Oxford**

# Contents

# List of Tables

Page

**Table**

# Preface

In 1994, we were intrigued by the rapid rise of the citizen militia movement, not only the speed with which the movement was spreading but also the strong convictions of those joining and leading the movement. As followers of social trends and as analyzers of human behavior in general, we were wondering, as sociologists often do, what social contexts underlay the rapid social changes we were observing.

Our first dilemma was that, although the phenomenon was intriguing and our curiosity was piqued as to causes, we thought initially that the phenomenon may have little to do with sociology. Perhaps political science was a better match, or the sociology of revolution is a subfield of sociology that might apply, but beyond that, there was not much substance for mainstream sociology. Adding to our dilemma was the fact that not much was written about the subject by sociologists. When it came to commentary and analysis on the movement, extremist watchers and journalists had contributed a great deal more than academic experts.

In the initial stages we pursued a literature review that gave us some ideas about how and where a program of empirical research might proceed. A preliminary proposal was drafted in 1996, and after substantial revisions, the final proposal was ready in 1999. During this time we put much effort into thinking about how the subject matter of citizen militias related to sociology, and that led us to the sociology of collective behavior and social movements, and ultimately, to Smelser's theory of collective behavior. Much of the data was collected in 1999-2000 as part of the senior author's doctoral dissertation. Supplemental data, including the interviews with militia people, were the last data collected, during 2001-2002.

We view documents posted to the Internet, when posted with conviction and good faith, to be legitimate objects for academic study. We found during the period 1994 to 2001 that many militia people were quite forthright about their opinions and set them into an electronic record with each posting that they contributed to the Usenet discussion groups. Their opinions as expressed in this Internet forum, we found out later, did not really differ much from what they say in interviews – when you can find a militia person that is willing to talk. We found, additionally, that a significant amount of items posted to the Usenet discussion groups were only tangentially related to militia issues or appeared to have little or no relationship to the militias. Perhaps that is why many militia people switched to more restricted environments such as the militia discussion group on Yahoo! by 2002. Given this development, we believe that we grasped a unique opportunity or window with which to study the public records of militia men and women.

As social movements form on the Internet and it becomes a forum and platform for those movements, we anticipate more opportunities for the kinds of research we have conducted here. We hope that this kind of research will continue to have the legitimacy and credibility that it deserves. To do otherwise would be to rob sociology and other social sciences of a rich source of textual data.

# Acknowledgments

We would like to thank the Shearman Research Initiative at McNeese State University for financial support that was granted to us during the 2001-2002 academic year. Such support enabled us to purchase an updated version of the technological tool that made this qualitative research relatively fairly easy: QSR-5. This tool saved us unnecessary hours of poring over the documents that were the primary data for this study. The study might have been conducted even without this generous gift, but the grant certainly expedited our work significantly and we are grateful for that.

Thanks are due as well to the two journals where earlier drafts of this research appeared: <u>Free Inquiry in Creative Sociology</u> and <u>The Sociological Quarterly</u>. The editors of these journals, John Cross and Kevin Leicht, respectively, were very generous in allowing our work to appear and we benefited greatly from the comments of the reviewers.

We are extremely grateful to University Press of America for eagerly embracing our work and validating it as worthy of publication. Many thanks are due to Stephen Ryan, UPA Acquisitions Editor, who expeditiously processed our initial inquiries; to UPA Vice President Judith Rothman who signed off on our work; and also to Beverly Baum who reviewed and provided comments on the formatting of the front matter and initial chapters, and generally guided us through the final stages. We are sure that there are many behind the scenes at UPA who contributed to our work – so many that we could not thank them all except to say warmheartedly, thanks for all your help.

Finally, many thanks go to our families for enduring our behavior during the writing phases and especially for allowing us the quiet time to complete this rigorous work. Without that endurance and patience, and without the time that was given to us, this project could not have been completed.

Stan C. Weeber
Daniel G. Rodeheaver
August 13, 2003

# Chapter 1

## Introduction

Sociologists, as data-gatherers, have been slow to show an interest in investigating the rise of the U.S. citizen militia movement in the 1990's. James Aho's now classic work on the Christian Patriots in the Pacific Northwest (1990, 1994) yielded rich qualitative data and set the stage for studies larger in scope: ones examining the social correlates of rates of militia activity and/or organizing (O'Brien and Haider-Markel, 1998; Van Dyke and Soule, 2002). More recently, in a handful of studies, militia people have been interviewed (Hoplight-Tapia, 2001; Albers, 2003; Gallaher, 2003). Unfortunately, to date, the field of sociology has offered little else in terms of sociological investigations yielding quantitative or qualitative data.

Sociologists have studied the right wing and revolutionary right from what can be described as a mostly theoretical social movement perspective (Berlet, 1995a; Diamond, 1995; Hamm, 1996; Dobratz and Shanks-Meile, 1997; Kaplan and Bjorno, 1998; Kaplan and Weinberg, 1998; Kimmel and Ferber, 2000; Katz and Bailey, 2000; Kaplan, 2000; Berlet and Lyons, 2000; Freilich, Pienik and Howard 2001; Nigel,

2001; Parish and Parker, 2001; Pitcavage, 2001; Crothers, 2002) or under the rubric of domestic terrorism (Turner, 2001), and some of the subjects studied were possibly militiamen or women, given that membership in extreme right groups often overlap (George and Wilcox, 1996). However, qualitative or quantitative data are lacking in these studies. Some, such as Dobratz and Shanks-Meile (1997), clearly state that their work is not specifically about persons in militias.

Consequently, sociologists had relatively little insight, based on data, to offer when militias burst upon the public scene following the Oklahoma City bombing. After the *New York Times* linked Timothy McVeigh and Terry Nichols to a citizen militia in northern Michigan, the public immediately made a strong linkage between the bombing suspects and the citizen militias. Subsequently, the militia movement was scrutinized in great detail by the press, politicians, law enforcement agencies, legal scholars and others. Legitimate concerns were raised that the militia movements' strong anti-government rhetoric contributed to an environment that may have encouraged the bombers to act (Berlet and Lyons, 1995; Stern, 1996). Connections between certain militiamen and various hate groups were exposed (Swomley, 1995), and militia members committed several terrorist acts after the bombing (DeArmond, 1995). The anthrax scare of 2001 brought attention to the possibility that U.S. militia people might be responsible. However, despite the significant impact of militias upon American society during the 1990's and beyond, militias are generally understudied by sociologists.


Why Do Militias Appear?


The overall lack of sociological interest is unexpected, given that sociologists have long been interested in the role that "anomie" or feelings of powerlessness play in peasant rebellions, protest movements, and related phenomena. Merton (1938) for instance contended that rebels, feeling the strain of living up to cultural goals and the established means of achieving them, reject and substitute both the culturally prescribed goals as well as the institutionalized means of achieving those goals. Smelser (1963) similarly approached revolutions and radical social movements from the standpoint of strain. He believed that people join radical movements because they experience social dislocation in the form of social strain, especially when such strain springs from rapid social change. These social movements reassure participants that something is being done to redress the underlying source of strain. Smelser (1963) asserted that four conditions follow the appearance of strain and that altogether, the five conditions he identified are necessary and sufficient conditions for radical social movements such as militias to occur.

Militias qualify as radical movements because of their strong anti-government rhetoric and general support for extreme measures to prevent what is often perceived as "America's slide into collectivism." Militia presence and activity on the Internet, then, is a phenomenon that can be studied within the framework of Smelser's theory. Militia watchers insist that those who join militias have experienced the kinds of social strains and other conditions to which Smelser refers (cf., Berlet and Lyons, 1995; Junas, 1995). Further, scholars argue that the Internet has become a forum for expressing such strains (Meador, 1996). The purpose of this study is to analyze the content of Internet traffic of U.S. militias in order to test Smelser's general thesis.


Internet and the Rise of Citizen Militias


Our study uses militia web sites and militia messages posted to Usenet as primary data to test Smelser's theory of collective behavior and this information, supplemented by interviews with militia people, will help to fill a critical research gap in our knowledge of citizen militias. It is also unique because it is one of the first sociological studies of militias that have an Internet presence (see also Weeber, 2001, and Donelan, 2001), and one of the first to study and collect primary data on militias from all regions of the U.S. Additionally, it is among the first sociological studies that provide a conceptual and operational definition of a citizen militia.

Aho's (1990) study of Idaho Christian Patriots demonstrated the promise of a qualitative study utilizing triangulated methods. His data consisted of phone and face-to-face interviews, questionnaires, and content analysis of movement literature. Because of the detail and depth that this work involved, he was restricted to studying Patriots and militia people within a relatively small geographic area, the state of Idaho. Although the current study being reported here also uses qualitative methods, this study is able to examine a larger group of subjects: people who joined militias from throughout the United States that had a web page or generated a significant amount of Internet discussion traffic. In order to triangulate information, interviews were conducted to supplement the primary data.

A basic assumption of our study is that use of Internet data can provide answers to the research questions posed. That is, web sites or messages posted by militiamen or women to Usenet discussion groups will provide answers to a series of questions that are important to Smelser's theory. For example, the data collected will help to reveal the underlying source of social strain potentially experienced by militia people, or will tell us about precipitating factors or about how social control affected the direction that the movement took after the Oklahoma City bombing.

A second assumption is that messages posted to the Internet are truthful indications of the militiaman or woman's state of mind and do reflect how that individual thinks and feels about issues considered important to militias in the United States. A very large proportion of militia people studied here was very forthright and signed their names to their messages. A much smaller percentage signed with a code name or an Internet "handle" that provided a slender, veiled disguise of their identity. It is assumed here that an unobtrusive study of Internet messages may actually give a more accurate picture of the average militia person's attitudes than a face-to-face interview, because of the reactivity that might be expected in an interview situation. The tendency of militia people to give inaccurate information in interviews has been documented (Lindstedt, 1997; Metcalf, 1998).


Defining Citizen Militias


A basic flaw of previous studies of citizen militias is the lack of an operationally useful definition of a citizen militia. In other words, researchers assumed they knew a militia when they saw it and did not see the need for a definition. Aho (1990) for example never defined the term "militia" in his classic study of Idaho patriots. Militiamen were a relatively small subset of the patriots he studied and he referred to them simply as "terrorists," a distinction that was clear to him and to his audience. Similarly, the Southern Poverty Law Center (1996, 1997) defined or labeled a group as a militia (with little or no elaboration or explanation) when they placed it on their watch list.

In this study, a citizen militia is conceptually defined as a private army that meets regularly to practice combat scenarios or skills and to discuss weapons. It may identify targets against which weapons could be used. A citizen militia may have an offensive, paramilitary orientation (seek and destroy) or a defensive orientation (e.g., protecting Americans from the New World Order) or both, depending upon circumstances (Stern, 1995).

A further distinguishing mark of a citizen militia is its reactionary, nostalgic, preservative nature. It tries to turn back the clock to a point in time that is perceived to have been better than the present. This kind of thinking has branched out in two different directions. First, the militia may see the "organic" constitution of the United States (the original articles plus the first ten amendments) as the "real" constitution, the one worth preserving at all costs. This is known as the Constitutional Republic that the militiamen want to protect (Sherwood, 1994).

A second line of thought, influenced by white supremacy and Christian Identity, is that the white race originated in the Garden of Eden and is now being preserved as part of a "new covenant" with God. Aryans replaced Jews as God's chosen people. (In contrast, minorities, gays/lesbians, liberals, and Jews are satanic enemies.) The role of the militia here is pro-active, to spark apocalyptic-like actions that will restore white men to their privileged position vis-à-vis their Creator (Aho, 1990; Mullins, 1993; Barkun, 1997).

Because this conceptual definition being used here is very broad, militias can be viewed as existing along a continuum in terms of their violence, tactics, and ideologies. At one end are well-organized and criminally effective terrorist groups such as The Order. This group specialized in covert action and was philosophically compatible with Christian Identity, neo-Nazism and kindred ideologies (Smith, 1994). The Order dissolved during the 1980s, but one militia studied here, the Aryan Republican Army, has been compared to The Order (Macko, 1996). Near the other extreme are public entities such as the Michigan Militia, whose orientations are primarily constitutionalist.

Furthermore, a citizen militia is operationally defined in this study as a group that: 1) puts combat scenarios/skills and weaponry plans into mock action, including in some cases going on maneuvers; 2) has an identifiable territory in which its members belong; 3) bases its organizational philosophies on anti-government rhetoric; 4) develops contingency plans in case of government provocation; 5) considers at least the viability of extreme measures to protect the organic constitution and/or white race such as bombings, kidnappings, separatism, and "paper terrorism"; and 6) considers, at minimum, the viability of criminal activity to gain weapons and explosives (Stern, 1995; George and Wilcox, 1996; Halpern and Levin, 1996; Duffy and Brantley, 1998). This definition insures that militias are social groups that practice skills within a distinct territory, are anti-government in outlook, and have definite opinions regarding use of terrorism to further militia goals.


## Summary and Plan of the Book


The aim of our book is to test, using a content analysis of the Internet traffic of U.S. militiamen supplemented by personal interviews, the thesis that social strain and other factors specified by Neil Smelser (1963) account for the rise of the most recent militia movement in the United States. Smelser's theory of collective behavior has been selected as the theoretical frame of reference because extant literature specific to U.S. militias (to be reviewed in Chapter 2), much of it from secondary sources, indicate that factors identified by Smelser played a role in the genesis and direction of this militia movement. Our study will view web sites and messages posted to the Internet as primary data to test Smelser's theory of collective behavior, helping to fill a critical research gap.

Chapter 2 reviews the literature on the evolution of citizen militias from the early republic to the neo-militia movement of the 1990s, the latter being of most importance to our study.

What is Smelser's theory of collective behavior? Because of its age, it is a classic social movement theory, but perhaps not one immediately recognized by today's students of sociology. Chapter 3 outlines and discusses Smelser's theory and applicability.

In Chapters 4 and 5 we discuss a unique way of getting information about a group of people who generally do not value social research or have any interest in it. We will use the vehicle that propelled the movement to public consciousness in the first place – the Internet – as the source of data for the study. We look at data sources, the sample, and the research questions that mostly parallel Smelser's theory.

Ultimately, we address the question: Is Smelser's theory supported by the data? In Chapters 6 and 7, we present the results of the study along with a discussion of the findings, in pursuant of an answer to this question.

We added Chapter 8 because some scholars remain unconvinced that the Internet is a legitimate source of data and that Internet-based data have little value in social research. In this chapter, we compare the results of 28 militias who do not have an Internet base with the 28 that do. In essence, how do these two types of militias differ?

In the final chapter, we "take the pulse" of the militia movement in the new millennium, and discuss where they might progress or digress as time progresses. We also discuss the implications of the results of the study for future research that utilizes Internet data, and also for future research in the area of militia studies.

# Chapter 2

---

# The Rise and Evolution of
# American Citizen Militias

The roots of the modern day militia movement lie in the revolutionary role of the militia in U.S. colonial history and the precedents for militias that appear in the Articles of Confederation, the Constitution, and subsequent federal legislation. Militias gained visibility, stature, and legitimacy by fighting at Lexington and later helped to repel the British advance on Concord. The value of militias to the developing republic of the United States was shown in the Articles of Confederation, where the early Congress was given the authority to call up the militia to quell invasions and the power to organize, arm, and discipline militias as needed to fulfill this purpose. After formulation of the U.S. republic, this authority and power was forwarded to Congress in Article 1, Section 8 of the U.S. Constitution. The Second Amendment further justified militias, stating that they were necessary to ensure a "free state." This amendment has been interpreted by some to mean that an important republican function of the militia is to safeguard against the tyranny of standing armies and government incumbents (Kates, 1983; Halbrook, 1984; Williams, 1991).


Militias in the New Republic


In the early 1800s, the federal government developed permanent military institutions, the most significant being a professional standing army. This shift to a professional army hastened the decline of the earliest militias, already suffering from poor training and equipment, and a shortage of men willing to engage in training. This essentially ended the nation's heavy reliance on militia units to perform vital functions (Hamilton, 1996).

When militias returned to the American scene in the 1860s, the circumstances were such that scholars highlighted anti-democratic tendencies in the militia and the pursuit of authoritarian goals (Berlet, 1995b). The public legitimacy and support granted to the earliest militias was now almost completely gone due to the violent tactics of the newer ones. For instance, the original Ku Klux Klan used murder, torture, rape, beatings, and arson to drive Black people back into subjugation and to restore White rule and planter control through the Democratic Party. This was in response to mass activism of Blacks and the limited but real gains achieved through Reconstruction (Berlet and Lyons, 2000). This "first era" of Klan activity was halted when President Ulysses S. Grant, under the authority of the Ku Klux Klan Act of April 1871, suspended the writ of habeas corpus in nine South Carolina counties. Authorities rounded up Klansmen and suspected Klansmen, holding some of them for long periods without formal charges. Some 1,250 Klansmen were convicted of various offenses, after which the Klan was disbanded (George and Wilcox, 1996).

The Klan's rebirth to a "second era" in 1915 followed widespread anxiety and fear of revolutionary leftists of the era. Prominent historians, writers and politicians of the era portrayed Reconstruction as a time of barbaric rule by Blacks and carpetbaggers, a time when the Klan nobly defended civilization and White womanhood (Berlet and Lyons, 2000; George and Wilcox, 1996).

The second era Klan, like the original group, was engaged in widespread violence. Vigilante activity was concentrated in five southern and southwestern states. In the fall of 1920, Klansmen paraded through southwestern towns to warn Blacks against voting. The Klan assaulted Blacks, Catholics, Jews, and immigrants for failing to be subservient, especially in the case of Black men, for purported insults given to White women. In September, 1921, a New York newspaper reported details of 152 attacks, including forty one whippings, twenty seven tar and featherings, and four murders (Berlet and Lyons, 2000). The Klan is also suspected to have organized the devastating 1921 Tulsa Riot in which hundreds of African Americans died in Tulsa's "Black Wall Street" commercial and residential district.

Following World War II, many in White America believed that societal order was under attack by Communists and Blacks, and some wondered if a connection existed between the two groups. Amid this concern, witch hunts began in search of enemies and their conspiratorial "evil" influences. Congress held hearings on domestic communism - most notably those led by Senator Joseph McCarthy - and labeled all leftists as "Reds." Civil rights leaders were not immune from such labeling; FBI Director J. Edgar Hoover strongly believed that an insidious connection existed, involving Martin Luther King and other civil rights activists, and the Communist movement (Hamilton, 1996).

Militias in the Early Modern Era

By 1960, fear of Communism assumed global proportions after Communist victories in China, Eastern Europe, Africa, and Latin America. As militias began to appear in the decade of the 1960s, the major concern was that there would be a collectivist takeover of the United States. Militias in general viewed themselves as drawing upon the old Colonial role of the militia as defenders of America against foreign invaders (Salsich, 1961). Beyond this similarity, however, early modern militias diverged philosophically along two different lines of thought. Some were constitutionalist in outlook (denoting a particular perspective and not a specific group) while others were influenced by Christian Identity, an ideology that first appeared in the U.S. in the 1870's. These are best viewed as ideal-typical philosophies or perspectives and not rigid categories. Each line of thought brought a definition to the collective force trying to dominate the United States.

Constitutionalists believed in the sanctity of the United States Constitution and contended that certain groups are conspiring to destroy America. They were reluctant to blame a definite ethnic, racial or religious category, favoring instead categories like "Bilderbergers," "Trilateralists," or "Force X" (Aho, 1990). Important in the early stages of constitutionalism was the encouragement and support it drew from tax protestors, the Posse Comitatus, the John Birch Society, and the Mormon Church.

Marvin Cooley's seminars in the early 1970's are often cited as the start of the tax protest movement. Cooley's seminars attracted future militiaman Robert Mathews, who would lead the terrorist militia The Order on a lawbreaking rampage a decade later. Formed by William Gale and Mike Beach in the late 1960's and later known as Posse Comitatus, the posse movement recognized the county sheriff as the highest legitimately elected official in the country and hoped to form local armed units that would compel government agents to obey the law of the U.S. Constitution. Gordon Kahl joined the Posse in the early 1970's and his death at the hands of North Dakota lawmen in 1983 was a precipitant of much militia-induced terrorism during the 1980's. The John Birch Society and the Mormon Church influenced the early lives of prominent constitutionalists, Robert DePugh, Robert Mathews, and Gordon Kahl. DePugh, for instance, belonged to the John Birch Society in the early years of the militia that he formed called the Minutemen. Mathews was motivated to attend Cooley's seminars after joining the Mormon Church and the John Birch Society while living with his parents in Phoenix (Jones, 1968; Aho, 1990; Corcoran, 1991; Flynn and Gerhardt, 1995; George and Wilcox, 1996).

Originating from the second line of thought, the Christian Identity ideology is built around three premises (Barkun, 1997). First, white Aryans are descendants of the biblical tribes of Israel and thus are on earth to do God's work. Second, Jews are completely unconnected to the Israelites and are actually children of the Devil, the literal biological offspring of a sexual relationship between Satan and Eve in the Garden of Eden. Finally, the world is on the verge of a final apocalyptic struggle between good and evil, in which Aryans must do battle with the Jewish conspiracy – an international conspiracy designed to destroy the United States – so that the world can be redeemed. Here, the "evil" collectivist force is international Jewry and its allies.

The American version of Christian Identity developed through C.A.L. Totten, Howard Rand and William Cameron; and, following a period of consolidation from 1936 until 1946, it grew rapidly on the West Coast with the preaching of Gerald L.K. Smith. Southern California was the vanguard of this ideology as several of Smith's protégés, including William Gale, preached and expanded upon the Christian Identity doctrine (Barkun, 1997).

Gale founded one of the early Christian Identity militias of the 1960's, the California Rangers. The Attorney General of California referred to the Rangers as an underground network for the conduct of guerilla warfare (State of California, 1965). It was Gale who introduced Richard Butler to Christian Identity leader Wesley Swift in the early 1960's. Butler was mesmerized by Swift's lectures and soon became a Christian Identity follower. He rose through the ranks quickly, leading a militia called the Christian Defense League. When Swift died in 1970, Butler took over Swift's congregation in Lancaster, California. Later, Butler would leave for northern Idaho, where he would help to establish a racially "pure" settlement around Hayden Lake and serve briefly as a mentor to Robert Mathews of The Order (Flynn and Gerhardt, 1995; Barkun, 1997).

Though some of the early militias could be classified as "constitutional," the predominant ideology of the early phase of the movement (from about 1960 to 1991) was based on that of Christian Identity. This was largely due to a popular and influential book (among militia members) by William Pierce called *The Turner Diaries* (1978). The book is a fictional account of a racist, anti-Semitic underground militia that, through a series of violent acts during the 1990's, gains power in America and eventually the world. The book describes the bombing of FBI headquarters in Washington, a mortar attack on the Capital building, the destruction of public utilities and communication systems, and the "liberation" of the nation after atomic bombs have been dropped on the East Coast. In the end, the U.S. population is reduced to 50 million Aryans (cf., Anti-Defamation League, 1995).

Pierce was not Christian Identity, but his book was widely read and admired by many that attended a 1982 meeting of right-wing organizations in northern Idaho, the purpose of which was to sign an Identity-inspired document called the Nehemiah Township Charter and Common Law Contract (Barkun, 1997). Believing that the "Zionist Occupational Government" had perverted the U.S. Constitution and the Declaration of Independence and that those two documents were no longer "covenants between God and Man," the Nehemiah Charter was considered the new covenant. It would become the Constitution under which the new government would rule after Armageddon. According to the Charter, Jesus Christ would lead the new government, whose purpose is to safeguard and protect the Christian faith. There would be no legislative body, no taxation, no governmental laws and only freemen (i.e., whites) would have personal freedoms according to a "Common Law" that is enforced by Posse Comitatus (Aho, 1990; Mullins, 1993).

Robert Mathews and Posse Comitatus leader Gordon Kahl were killed in shoot-outs with police during the 1980's. Later that decade, ten militia leaders were charged with sedition and put on trial in Fort Smith, Arkansas. Essentially, this rendered the movement financially and ideologically bankrupt. Consequently, there was a lull in militia activity until after the standoff between the Bureau of Alcohol, Tobacco and Firearms (BATF) and the Branch Davidians in Waco in 1993.

Though some note continuity between the early phase of the militia movement and the one to follow – due largely to a meeting at Estes Park, Colorado in October, 1992 (cf., Dees and Corcoran, 1997) - there is literature which also suggests that the 1990's movement is something new and different, and is not influenced as much by the earlier phase (Schneider, 1994; Berlet and Lyons, 1995; Wills, 1995). Either way, whether or not Christian Identity doctrine or constitutionalism is the leading paradigm guiding the most recent movement is in question.


The Neo-Militia Movement of the 1990's


In the neo-militia movement of the 1990s (defined as the movement that began in the United States around 1992 and continues to the present), some constitutionalist themes are present along with some underlying Christian Identity themes (Robertson, 1991; Aho, 1994; Helvarg, 1995). The literature does not conclusively answer the question of which kind of theme is predominant (Weeber, 1999). Consequently, the question of whether or not the neo-militia movement flows directly from the white supremacist movement or is something distinctly detached from it is a question that could not be answered from the literature review.

That being said, it is nonetheless possible to draw out some themes with respect to the origins of this most recent phase of the militia movement. Underlying the movement are distrust of and a general dissatisfaction with the encroachment of the federal government into the lives of American citizens, and the perceived erosion of constitutional republicanism. For instance, John Trochmann of the Militia of Montana said that his mission was to make people aware of the "military takeover" of the U.S. and how constitutional freedoms were being eroded, especially the right to keep and bear arms (Barkun, 1997).

Beyond the general dissatisfaction noted by Trochmann and other militiamen, the new militia (or neo-militia) movement draws its strength from and is supportive of a number of right wing causes. In general, militias oppose the U.S. Federal Reserve and federal tax system, are protective of property rights, believe in "judicial purity" (e.g., juries should not allow judges to instruct them, because jury members have power to determine points of law and evidence) and object to the bullying of the politically unorthodox by police agencies (*Dallas Morning News*, 1994; Helvarg, 1995; Wills, 1995). Thus, there is some carryover of the constitutionalist themes that were evident in some of the early militias of the modern era.

Furthermore, these neo-militias object to government interference in education, abortion policy, and the environment, and believe that it is time to roll back the clock on these issues. Interestingly, mainstream conservative views on these issues are quite similar to those of the neo-militias (Schneider, 1994; Halpern and Levin, 1996).

In the minds of many militia members, two events seem to hallmark the shift in the winds of change, altering the role of the U.S. federal government in the lives of average American citizens. These are the standoff at the Randy Weaver home in Ruby Ridge, Idaho, and the one at the Branch Davidian complex in Waco, Texas. Because of their importance, these two events will be discussed in detail in chapter 3.

However, even before these two important events, two others are cited by militiamen as being significant. First is a 1990 speech by President George Bush in which he declared a new world order in which all countries of the world would compete economically but cooperate in peacekeeping missions under the authority of the U.N (Walker, 1994; Halpern and Levin, 1996).

Others point to Pat Robertson's *The New World Order* (1991) as a key turning point (*Church and State*, 1995). In this book, he argues that a tightly knit international cabal, beginning with the Illuminati and Freemasons and continued with communism and late-capitalist high finance, is trying to establish a new order of the human race under the domination of Lucifer and his followers. This new order today is guided by the same "evil" influences that have guided it for centuries (Aho, 1990).

## Summary

In early America militias gained visibility and stature as well as public legitimacy by virtue of their successful performance at Lexington and Concord and the subsequent legislation that justified by existence of citizen militias. With the establishment of a professional standing army, however, the nation's heavy reliance on militia units to perform vital functions all but ended.

In the next historical stage, militias appear to lack public support because of the violent tactics they used; for example, the first and second eras of the Ku Klux Klan. In general, the militias that emerged early in the modern era (1960-1991) drew upon the old Colonial and classic republican tradition of an unorganized, armed populace. Though sharing this common background and organizing theme, this early movement gave rise to two differing philosophies, constitutionalism and Christian Identity, with the latter predominating.

The movement that emerged in the 1990s is much more difficult to characterize according to its primary ideological content, drawing themes from both constitutionalism and Christian Identity.

Chapter 3

---

# Smelser's Theory of
# Collective Behavior

As noted at the outset of our study, though sociologists have done a fair amount of conceptual thinking about the revolutionary right and the right-wing in general, there is a definite shortage of sociological data specific to U.S. militias. It should also be pointed out that an ample amount of the literature that we do have on the evolution of American militias, and in particular that on the neo-militia movement, has been authored by journalists, historians, and others who are not sociologists and, therefore, the research has not been formulated or interpreted from a sociological point of view. A good deal of the literature reviewed in the previous chapter bears the imprint of this influence, being mostly socio-historically descriptive and putting emphasis on the development of certain key leaders of the movement and their impact upon the movement as a whole. Sociologically, Smelser's theory of collective behavior provides a more useful paradigm because it helps explain the underlying factors that might have lead to the genesis of the neo-militia movement in the early 1990's, and it is testable: data can be gathered to see if the theory is an adequate explanation for the genesis of the most recent movement.

Smelser's theory is over thirty years old and the question could be legitimately raised as to why such an old theory can be considered relevant to a recent phenomenon such as the citizen militia movement. Garner and Tenuto (1997), in their review of the social movement literature describe Smelser's theory as a bridge between an initial phase in the literature that emphasized irrational aspects of collective behavior and a second phase that was more sociological in outlook. Currently, a third "postmodern" phase has emerged. So, the question again might be posed as to why Smelser's theory could be relevant now if it is part of a tradition in social movement theory whose most productive days are in the past.

Simply put, Smelser's theory is the best fit between what observers have seen (empirically) of the movement so far and a logical explanation for the movement's genesis. In other words, it is the best match between current information that we have, much of it from secondary sources, and a theoretical explanation for it. Furthermore, there are similarities between the current movement and the kinds of right-wing extremism that existed when Smelser wrote. Considering these factors, Smelser's theory appears to be the most powerful explanation that we have for the rise of the 1990's militia movement. In this study we put this idea to the test.


## Smelser's Model


Smelser's theory of collective behavior (1963) is a general theory that accounts for the development of various kinds of collective behavior, social movements being only one type. It is often referred to as one of the classical social movement theories, and has one preliminary point followed by five main points.

The preliminary point is that a social structure must be conducive or permissive of a certain kind of collective behavior. A money market, for instance, even though its structure is conducive to panic, may function for long periods without producing a crisis. Within the scope of a conducive structure, many possible kinds of behavior other than panic remain. Similarly, in a free democratic nation such as the United States, the social structure is conducive to many possible kinds of behavior other than radical social movements, and permits them along with other kinds of behavior. For example, the right to freedom of assembly and freedom of association that appear in the U.S. Constitution are conducive to the formulation of militias as well as other kinds of social groups or movements. More specifically, modern day militias draw upon colonial history and the precedents for militias that appear in the Articles of Confederation, the Constitution, and subsequent federal legislation – the Militia Act of 1903, the National Defense Act of 1916, and Section 10 of the U.S. Code (U.S. Senate, 1982; Hardy, 1985). Militias today see themselves (and not the National Guard) as the militia mandated in these laws and as protectors of the people against an arrogant, tyrannical government. The U.S. social structure allowed for these legislative landmarks which in turn allow the militias to see themselves as legitimate players in the defense of America.

Realizing that a social structure may be conducive to a wide range of behavioral possibilities, Smelser (1963) added several more determinants that make it ever more probable that a particular type of collective behavior would emerge.

First, he believed that underlying social strain must be present for a social movement to occur. Smelser defined strain as the impairment of the relations among, and consequent inadequate function of, the components of social action. Following Parsons and Shils (1951), Smelser defined the four components as values, norms, mobilization into organized roles (social structures) and situational facilities (actor's knowledge of the opportunities and limitations of the environment). These are arranged in a hierarchy with values ranked highest and facilities lowest. Furthermore, moving from the top to the bottom of the hierarchy, concrete details of action receive increasingly more specific definition.

Smelser believed that strain in a social system will show itself at a lower, more operative level, such as mobilization into organized roles or situational facilities. Then, once this strain appears at this lower level, a search for the reasons for the strain begins to call into action the higher levels. Smelser's view was that strain could manifest itself in many ways, strains could cluster together in unusual ways, and the relationships between multiple strains could be complex.

Smelser did see a correlation between certain types of strain and certain types of collective behavior. He notes that value-oriented beliefs (the kind found in a militia movement) may arise under conditions of severe physical deprivation or economic hardship as was the case in the millenarian movements in the late Middle Ages. Here, the strain is a psychological state of the individual as well as an objective condition that observers can see.

Recent research shows a similar link between deprivation and the rise of right-wing activity. Weinberg (1993) for example contends that the radical right (including militias) of the 1980s drew members from economically distressed sectors of the economy. Due to global corporate restructuring, the number of employed Americans whose incomes fell below the poverty line rose 23 percent from 1978 through 1987. The principal losers in this trend, who felt a real decline in their earning power, were those workers engaged in routine production services (e.g., farming, manufacturing) and those who provide routine personal services such as truck drivers, custodians, restaurant employees, and barbers.

Adding to this real deprivation was the relative deprivation suffered by some Whites as their status in the world was declining relative to other racial categories in society. In particular, there was an undercurrent of resentment against what are seen as the unfair advantages the government gives to people of color and Women. In the eyes of these Whites, these advantages are the result of the feminist and civil rights movements; civil rights legislation and court decisions; welfare; affirmative action programs; and educational programs for the economically disadvantaged that exclude nonminorities (Berlet and Lyons, 1995).

There is another kind of strain that correlates with the behavior of radical social movements such as militias. Smelser (1963) writes that inadequacy of knowledge or techniques to grapple with new situations sets the stage for value-oriented movements. Value-oriented beliefs are not a simple function of superstition or lack of knowledge; the inadequacy of facilities to explain unusual events or cope with situational problems does, however, contribute to the rise of these, rather than other types of movements. For instance, Bell (1963) wrote that the radical right of the early 1960s, including some militias, arose due the inability to comprehend "modernity," or the belief in rational assessment, rather than established custom, for the evaluation of social change. Furthermore, this modernity was a bellwether in the fading dominance of custom, once exercised through the institutions of small-town America. Moreover, a similar inability to comprehend a "post-modernity" in which prior rational assessments were no longer guideposts for understanding rapid social change, may have been important in the rise of the patriot movement and especially the constitutional neo-militias of the 1990s (McAlvany, 1990). Giddens (1994) further argued that the complexities of postmodern globalization may have led to the development of recent political and religious fundamentalisms.

Second, Smelser posits a generalized belief that identifies the source of strain and at least suggests certain lines of actions as being appropriate to remedy the source of the strain. This is, in Smelser's terms, the search for explanation of the source of strain at a higher level of social action, i.e., norms and values. Among future militiamen, at least one such generalized belief called the "New World Order," began to circulate in the early 1990s, just before the appearance of the movement (Stern 1995, 1996). This generalized belief stimulated thoughts about how to contain this new threat and the types of action that might need to be taken. According to this idea, a U.N.-led force was poised to take over the United States and administer a totalitarian, collectivist government (Ridgeway and Zeskind, 1995; U.S. Senate, 1997; Pitcavage, 2001). The socialism of the old Soviet Union had not died; it had simply been transferred to the United Nations. Fear of this new threat of collectivism was the militias' "call to arms," and devotees thought that they must bear arms and train to resist an impending takeover (Schneider, 1994; Cockburn, 1995; McFadden, 1995).

Third, Smelser contended that hastening or precipitating events must confirm the generalized belief before the movement can appear. These events create, sharpen, or exaggerate a condition of strain, and link the generalized belief to concrete situations. By doing so, a movement becomes closer to actualization. The perceived heavy-handed treatment of U.S. citizens by government agents in Ruby Ridge, Idaho, and Waco, Texas, reinforced the imagery of the New World Order and, according to some, helped precipitate the neo-militia movement (Barkun, 1997; Hamm, 1997). At Ruby Ridge, Randy Weaver had been indicted for selling illegal shotguns to an informant and refused to appear in court. This led to a tense, controversial standoff between Weaver and a force of U.S. Marshals, FBI and ATF agents, during which Weaver's wife Vicki and son Sammy were shot and killed. At Waco, a raid by ATF agents at the compound of a religious sect called the Branch Davidians resulted in a shootout followed by a 51-day standoff. This standoff ended with a fire in which 76 Branch Davidians died.

Fourth, Smelser believed that leaders emerge to give the fledgling movement a sense of direction. Following Weber (1947), he believed that leaders in a value-oriented movement such as a militia would be charismatic, with exceptional powers or qualities. Because a value-oriented movement calls for a reconstruction of the entire social order, a diffuse, total kind of commitment is needed. Charismatic leadership is, then, the most generalized form of leadership, for in such a leader is placed the hopes for a collective reconstitution of values. Several charismatic leaders (Jon Roland, Bob Fletcher, Bo Gritz, J.J. Johnson, Martin Lindstedt, Linda Thompson) played a role in mobilizing the neo-militia movement, and along the way, demonstrated a sophisticated use of the Internet as a tool to assist in movement mobilization (e.g., Texas Militia Papers 1996; Meador 1996).

Finally, social control mechanisms initiated by elites in power affects the direction of the movement once it has started. Smelser (1963) believed that a value-oriented movement, once crystallized, has a potential for moving in many directions - it may come to naught; it may form into a cult or a sect, it may go underground, or it may turn into a revolutionary force. A major determinant of the movement's course lies in the behavior of agencies of social control in response to the movement. According to some analysts, the official response to the militia movement in the U.S. in the form of anti-terrorism legislation and negative press drove a significant proportion of the movement underground (Southern Poverty Law Center, 1996), one of the possibilities suggested by Smelser.

The studies cited in this section to support the application of Smelser's theory to neo-militias are secondary sources. Thus, a summary statement would be that Smelser's theory is supported by secondary sources but has yet to be tested with primary data with respect to the militia phenomenon in the United States.


Criticisms of Smelser's Theory


Several competing theories rose to challenge Smelser's. Resource mobilization theory (developed mostly to overcome perceived weaknesses in the social strain approach) emphasizes that social movements should be seen as rational, goal-oriented efforts to engage in political conflict for realistic advantages. According to this view, protests may be the only way in which groups excluded from established institutions can fight effectively for their interests. Strain may not be necessary in these circumstances, in that there are always social strains and conflicts of interest built into existing social arrangements. But often less powerful groups are too atomized or demoralized to form a social movement. Thus, this approach emphasizes the element of time that it takes for atomized or disconnected aggrieved people to form associations with one another. For resource mobilization theorists, potentially aggrieved groups must achieve some degree of solidarity in order to act; and preexisting social networks or organizations are likely to be involved in launching social movements (Skocpol and Campbell, 1995).

Another alternative, Marxist theories, argued that the formation of social movements is tied to capitalist social structure (cf., O'Connor, 1973). Recent work by Reich (2001) points out how even at higher reaches of the pay scale there is economic stress due to job insecurity, declining wages, and additional hours worked. Threats to well being need not be purely economic, but may be psychological as well. This argument points toward a progressive slide of the seemingly well off into a Marxian "working class" and implies, at least, that a two class model has some viability in explaining a phenomenon such as the militias, whose membership is believed to be predominantly middle class (Keen, 1998; Kushner, 1998; Snow, 1999). Thus, one might be able to argue that the militias are indeed a class phenomenon and have middle or working class interests diametrically opposed to a ruling class in a two-class system.

The political opportunities model of McAdam (1982) tried to tap the strengths but also improve upon the weaknesses of both the classical and resource mobilization approaches. It is a process model, like Smelser's, and also is concerned with the degree to which organizations are ready and able to provide support for a movement. The political process model identifies three sets of factors that are believed to be crucial in the generation of social insurgency. The first is the level of organization within the aggrieved population (degree of organizational "readiness"); the second is the collective assessment of the prospects for successful insurgency within that same population (level of "insurgent consciousness" within the mass base of the movement); and the third is the political alignment of groups within the larger political environment (the structure of political opportunities available to insurgent groups). The concern with degree of readiness of insurgent groups reflects the concern with the time element that is explicit in resource mobilization theory and the importance that preexisting networks may play in this process.

Snow and his colleagues (1986) have taken a different track, choosing to refine and extend our understanding of the cognitive basis of collective action by proposing a typology of "frame alignment processes" by which activists seek to construct legitimating accounts to support their own and others' activism (see discussion in McAdam, McCarthy and Zald, 1988). New movements always entail some break with established behavioral routines. In order to overcome people's natural reluctance to break with these routines, ideological rationales must be fashioned that legitimate the movement's behavioral proscriptions. Snow and colleagues distinguish four distinct frame alignment processes – frame bridging, frame amplification, frame extension, and frame transformation - by which these rationales are constructed.

Despite the worthy and viable alternative theories to choose from, we continue to believe that Smelser's framework has potential utility in explaining and predicting militia behavior. His theory provides a good match with the available secondary source information, and it provides a theoretically grounded, logical and temporal explanation for the appearance of the militia movement. Furthermore, if the theory is validated by primary data, it could assist social scientists in predicting the next wave of militia activity.


Summary


Though sociologists have done a fair amount of conceptual thinking about the revolutionary right and the right-wing in general, there is a definite shortage of sociological data collected about U.S. militias. Some of the important information that we do have has been authored by non-sociologists. Sociologically speaking, Smelser's theory of collective behavior provides a more useful paradigm because it helps explain the underlying factors that might have lead to the genesis of the neo-militia movement.

Smelser's theory is over thirty years old and the question could be legitimately raised as to why this theory can be considered a relevant one today. Simply put, the theory is the best fit between what observers have seen of the movement so far and a logical explanation for the movement's genesis.

Smelser's theory is a general theory that accounts for the development of various kinds of collective behavior, social movements being only one type. It has one preliminary point followed by five main points.

The preliminary point is that a social structure must be conducive or permissive of a certain kind of collective behavior. The first major point is that social strain of some kind must be present for a social movement to occur. Second, at least one generalized belief must emerge that identifies the source of strain and at minimum, suggests certain lines of action as being appropriate to remedy the source of the strain. Third, precipitating events must confirm the generalized belief before the movement can appear. Fourth, leaders emerge to give the fledgling movement a sense of direction. Fifth, social control mechanisms initiated by elites in power affects the direction of the movement once it has started.

The studies cited in this chapter to support the application of Smelser's theory to neo-militias are secondary sources. Thus, a summary statement would be that Smelser's theory is supported by secondary sources but has yet to be tested with primary data with respect to the militia phenomenon in the United States.

Though having its critics, Neil Smelser's theory of collective behavior remains the most useful explanation that we could find for the rise of the 1990's citizen militias. It provides a framework that has potential utility in explaining and predicting militia behavior. His theory provides a theoretically grounded, logical and temporal explanation for the appearance of the movement. Furthermore, if the theory could be shown to be empirically relevant to the neo-militia movement it could assist social scientists in predicting the next wave of militia activity.

Chapter 4

# Testing Smelser's Theory:
# Data Sources and Sample Selection

Smelser's theory will be tested in this study by analyzing the content of Internet traffic of U.S. neo-militias. This includes a content analysis of relevant web pages and Usenet traffic. Each message or page was scrutinized carefully for both its manifest and latent content (Babbie, 1995). Content analysis as a research design has the advantage of allowing the researcher the opportunity to peruse the message an unlimited number of times, whereas in observational studies or interviews, the observer's memory and note taking skills are called into play as key variables in the data gathering process. Additionally, an unobtrusive study of Internet traffic avoids the problem of reactivity that might be expected in studying militiamen and women.

Data Sources

The data for this study were drawn from a preliminary list of 244 militias identified during August, 1998, from a number of sources: the Southern Poverty Law Center (1996, 1997), John Whitley (1998), and a systematic browsing of the Internet, the *New York Times Index*, and First Search. The final list of militias to be studied was determined by screening each of the militias on the preliminary list against the operational definition of a citizen militia as it was defined in this study. Then, for each militia that met the operational definition, that particular militia was checked to see if it had a web site or if it had generated a significant amount of Usenet traffic. This procedure identified 28 militias in five regions of the U.S. (see Table 1). A total of 171 militiamen/women were studied who belonged to the 28 identified militias (see Table 2). Each research subject was assigned a case number; all but one can be identified by name.

Of the 28 militias studied, 7 were from the Southeast, 9 from the West, 7 from the Midwest, 3 from the Southwest and 2 from the East. As for the militiamen and women who belonged to these militias, 19 were from the Southeast, 33 were from the West, 42 were from the Midwest, 69 were from the Southwest, and 8 were from the East. Compared with a group of 132 militias studied by the Southern Poverty Law Center in 1998 (see Table 3), our sample is slightly over represented with militias from the West and is under represented by Midwestern and Eastern militias.

Nearly all the subjects were men (97%), and, though data on ethnic group identity were not generally available nor could be inferred from most messages posted, we do know that at least two subjects were African American and one was Jewish. The remainder is probably White, based on an examination of subjects' surnames together with the observations about ethnicity made by the "watch" organizations (Southern Poverty Law Center, 1996).

Occupational data were available for 54 of the militiamen or women. These are self-reported data as well as data that are reported by militia leaders or occupations attributed to militiamen or women by their peers. We have no reason to believe at this time that these data are any more or less reliable than other kinds of self-reported occupational data. Professionals or managers accounted for 52.5 percent of the total; sales, technical and administrative for 17 percent; manual labor for 22 percent; and low skill and service workers made up 8.5 percent of the

**Table 1**
**Militias Studied by Region**

| Region | Militia |
| --- | --- |
| *Southeast* | Alabama Constitutional Militia |
| | Florida State Militia |
| | Gadsden Minutemen (AL) |
| | Georgia Militia |
| | Northwest Florida Militia |
| | Sons of Liberty (AL) |
| | 91$^{st}$ Brigade (NC) |
| *West* | Cascade Brigade (WA) |
| | Colorado 1$^{st}$ Light Infantry |
| | Colorado Minutemen |
| | Militia of Arizona |
| | Militia of Montana |
| | San Diego Militia (CA) |
| | Southern Oregon Militia |
| | Viper Militia (AZ) |
| | Washington State Militia |
| *Midwest* | Aryan Republican Army |
| | Michigan Militia Corps |
| | North American Militia (MI) |
| | Northern Illinois Minutemen |
| | Ohio Unorganized Militia |
| | 7$^{th}$ Missouri Militia |
| | 51$^{st}$ Missouri Militia |
| *Southwest* | New Mexico Militia |
| | Oklahoma Constitutional Militia |
| | Texas Constitutional Militia |
| *East* | Blue Ridge Hunt Club (VA) |
| | West Virginia Mountaineer Militia |

**Table 2**
**Internet Militia Cases Studied by Region**

| Region | Number of Cases | Case Numbers | Percent of Total Cases |
|---|---|---|---|
| Southeast | 19 | 1-19 | 11.11 |
| West | 33 | 20-52 | 19.30 |
| Midwest | 42 | 53-94 | 24.56 |
| Southwest | 69 | 95-163 | 40.35 |
| East | 8 | 164-171 | 4.68 |
| Total | 171 | | 100.00 |

**Table 3**
**A Comparison of Internet Versus SPLC Militias by Region**

| Region | Internet Militias | | SPLC Militias* | |
|---|---|---|---|---|
| | Number | Percent | Number | Percent |
| Southeast | 7 | 25 | 32 | 24 |
| West | 9 | 32 | 28 | 21 |
| Midwest | 7 | 25 | 44 | 33 |
| Southwest | 3 | 10 | 9 | 7 |
| East | 2 | 7 | 19 | 14 |
| Total | 28 | 100 | 132 | 100 |

Note:     *Source: Southern Poverty Law Center (1998).

total. Leaders accounted for 19 percent of the total subjects studied and followers, 81 percent.

All research subjects had access to Usenet, a discussion system that is distributed worldwide. It consists of a set of news groups with names that are classified by subject. Messages are "posted" to these news groups by people on computers with the appropriate software. Consequently, Usenet is not a bulletin board, listserv or "chat line." The Usenet archive, <u>Deja News</u>, saved all messages posted until being taken over by Google in February, 2001.

Most subjects signed their names to the messages. Therefore, we were able to sort through all the messages for each subject to observe writing styles and message content, and it was very obvious when an imposter tried to claim the identity of one of the regular posters, given the vehement negative response of that regular poster. We actually got to "know" the people through their messages and style of presentation, and we felt that enough of a paper trail was left that we could state that these were real militiamen or women with strong convictions.

Additionally, many of these individuals posting to Usenet were already publicly identified by "watch" organizations or by public proclamations on Usenet announcing regional leaders of some of the militias studied. This further supports the idea that the militiamen and women were actual people and not anonymous individuals posting and then leaving the newsgroup.

Thus, the question, "Who are these people?" is not an issue at all. All but one can be identified by name, so the real issue is how the names of these subjects can be kept confidential. While it cannot be verified beyond a reasonable doubt that each and every message posted was posted by a militiaman or woman (and not a federal agent, scholar, extremist watcher, or other interested party), the high volume of messages posted by many subjects together with the highly emotional content of several of the messages would appear to weigh against the probability that participation is based purely upon the pecuniary or professional considerations that might be the top priority of an agent that is infiltrating the group.

## Representativeness of the Sample

Several questions could be raised about the representativeness of the sample. Does this study look at a socio-economically more affluent subset of the militia movement because it is limited to militiamen/women who own a computer and have the technological capability to post to the Internet? This would suggest a higher level of intelligence and possibly more income than other militiamen or women. Thus, are the message posters truly representative of a broader group of militia members who may or may not use the Internet? Is the Internet user group a unique subset of all militia members, a distinctive set of leaders, or more typical of the "average" militia member?

Evidence suggests that many who joined militias in the 1990s already had computer knowledge and competency due to their participation in computer bulletin board systems (BBS). A BBS is a freestanding computer system that is tied to one or more phone lines. Dial-in users can exchange text files and messages. Virtually anyone with a computer, a modem and a phone line could hook up to the bulletin board. Technological savvy was not required, nor was state of the art equipment; old, second hand equipment, the kind that could be purchased at pawnshops, was entirely adequate. Moreover, some of the bulletin board systems were quite popular en masse. The Paul Revere Network that began in 1987 connected thousands of patriots as did Liberty Net, Patriot Net, Spirit of '76, Associated Electronic News, and other bulletin boards.

The mass strength of these patriot networks was first evident during the 1992 presidential campaign of Ross Perot. As Berlet (2001) notes, libertarians and populist conservatives, who appear to have strongly influenced the politics of early cyber-culture and later the Internet, helped circulate organizing documents and position papers for the Perot campaign, quickly reaching a large audience. Perot's anti-government themes also attracted support from some persons in the extremist right who later went on to promote the patriot and militia movements (Berlet, 2001).

According to Berlet (2001), these pre-existing online relationships were a factor in the subsequent use of computer networks by the patriot and militia movements. A very large amount of information and numerous discussions about tactics and strategy for the militia and patriot movements moved across the Internet, appearing in Usenet newsgroup conferences such as alt.conspiracy, talk.politics.guns, alt.sovereignty, misc.survivalism, alt.politics.usa.constitution, and ultimately, misc.activism.militia. In short, those who were posting to militia Usenet groups by the mid 1990s, both leaders and rank and file, had been plugged into computers for about 10 years. Their participation was more a matter of ideological commitment than of occupation, income, or technical knowledge.

Relevant information from web sites and Usenet postings by or about the selected militias and militiamen was downloaded to diskettes from September 1, 1998 to August 22, 2001. Overall, 6,285 on-line documents were downloaded to disks for analysis. Of these, there were 1,196 which had sufficient content to answer one or more of the research questions. Because one document could have information relevant to more than one research question, there are a total of 1,249 messages that were related to the six research questions posed in this study.

The downloaded information was converted to Microsoft Word files, then Nonnumerical Unstructured Data Indexing Searching and Theorizing (NUDIST) was used to assist with the data analysis (Qualitative Data Solutions, 1994). This software package was programmed to look for keywords and chunks of text (the sentences prior to and after the keyword) that pertain to the six research questions, and then generated a report related to each keyword.

The reports produced by NUDIST indicated the files that might be germane to each of the research questions. Each of these files was then checked and each document that helped to answer any of the research questions was examined for its manifest and latent content, and coded according to instructions that appeared in the codebook of the principal investigator. Smelser's theory, as a process model, would be considered falsified if there is little or no evidence to answer any one of the research questions.


Summary


This study employs content analysis to study the Internet postings and web pages of U.S. militiamen and women to determine with primary data whether Smelser's theory of collective behavior is an adequate tool to explain the rise of the militia movement in the U.S. during the 1990s. Content analysis has the advantage of allowing the researcher the opportunity to peruse the message an unlimited number of times, whereas in observational studies, the observer's memory and note taking skills are called into play in the data gathering process.

The data for the study were drawn from a preliminary list of 244 militias identified in August, 1998 as candidates for study. After this list was screened against an operational and conceptual definition of a citizen militia, only 28 militias remained. Essentially, only these 28 militias had a Web or Usenet presence that was sufficient enough to study. A total of 171 militiamen and women that belong to these militias were the subjects studied.

Relevant information from web sites and Usenet postings by or about the selected militias and militiamen was downloaded to diskettes from September 1, 1998 to August 22, 2001. Overall, 6,285 on-line documents were downloaded to disks for analysis. Of these, there were 1,196 which had sufficient content to answer one or more of the research questions.

The downloaded information was converted to Microsoft Word files, then Nonnumerical Unstructured Data Indexing Searching and Theorizing (NUDIST) was used to assist with the data analysis. This software program searched for key words in the textual documents (i.e. Internet messages and web pages) and then information relevant to the research questions was coded and prepared for analysis.

Chapter 5

# Testing Smelser's Theory:
# Variables and Research Questions

Table 4 provides a visual overview of Smelser's theory. In it, we provide a brief description of the major ideas in Smelser's theory. The preliminary point of the theory is not tested in our study because freedom of speech and assembly is guaranteed in the U.S. Constitution, and thus the U.S. social structure is conducive to the development of citizen militias and other kinds of social movements. One could argue that the mere appearance of the movement alone was evidence of conduciveness.

Second, we argue that there is structural conduciveness because of the structure of computer bulletin boards that allowed for open communication and set the stage for the development of the militias utilizing the Internet as an organizing principle. The discussion below documents the remaining variables and research questions.

### Table 4
### An Overview of Smelser's Theory of Collective Behavior

Preliminary Point:    A social structure must be ***conducive*** or permissive of a certain kind of collective behavior or social movement.

Major Point 1:    Underlying ***social strain*** must be present for a social movement to occur.

Major Point 2:    At least one ***generalized belief*** must appear that identifies the source of strain and suggests certain lines of action as being appropriate to remedy the source of the strain.

Major Point 3:    ***Precipitating events*** must confirm the generalized belief before the movement can appear.

Major Point 4:    Leaders engage in a ***mobilization for action*** that gives the fledgling movement a sense of direction.

Major Point 5:    ***Social control*** mechanisms initiated by elites in power affects the direction of the movement once it has started. A value-oriented movement has potential to move in many directions – it may come to naught; it may form into a cult or a sect; it may go underground; or it may turn into a revolutionary force.

Structural Strain

Smelser (1963) argues that structural strain is a precondition for the development of a social movement. Considering that extremist watchers have identified strains similar to those mentioned by Smelser, (cf., Berlet and Lyons, 1995; Junas, 1995) the question to be answered is: Did militiamen/women experience strain prior to or during their tenure in the militia?

Smelser delineated four types of strain that he believed would be most common as a precondition for a social movement; however, he eventually concedes that any kind of strain can produce any kind of movement. Consequently, in this study the decision was made not to exclude any kinds of strains that might be reported by or for militiamen or women. (See Appendix E for detailed documentation on the coding of all variables).


Generalized Beliefs


According to Smelser (1963), strain alone was not sufficient for a social movement to appear; it must be accompanied by at least one generalized belief that puts the participant's stress into a context and gives an explanation for the kinds of stress being experienced. Given that the literature documents the appearance of a belief called the New World Order (cf., Stern, 1996), the relevant question is: Before joining the militia, or during militia membership, were militiamen or women introduced to the idea of the New World Order, and did they accept it?

In this study, messages whose manifest and latent content indicated that the militiaman or woman had accepted the concept of the New World Order prior to or during militia membership were coded as indicating support for that particular generalized belief. This includes explicit remarks by individuals indicating acceptance of the New World Order or support as inferred from individual remarks and group statements or declarations. Nonsupport for the New World Order was noted in militia messages where there was no acceptance of this generalized belief as a frame of reference for understanding the kinds of stress experienced. This includes explicit remarks that this belief is not important (e.g., "we do not think about the NWO, this is an urban myth perpetuated by the media"), or explicit comments that other kinds of concepts may be more important (e.g.," [instead of militias being concerned with NWO] most are mainly concerned with getting the Federal Government down to a manageable size…), or the same result as inferred implicitly from remarks posted (e.g., the Alabama Declaration that was signed by several militiamen and women in support of constitutionalist principles contains no references at all to NWO).

### Precipitating Events

The existence of strain accompanied by generalized beliefs is not enough to produce an episode of collective behavior, according to Smelser (1963). Precipitating events are crucial. These events confirm the explanations for stress contained within the generalized belief and crystallize calls for action. Some writers contend that certain important events precipitated the rise of the neo-militia movement (cf., Stern, 1996), so the research question is: Were events at Ruby Ridge and Waco, together with the passage of gun control legislation, important reasons why participants joined the militia?

### Mobilization for Action

Given the appearance of strain, generalized beliefs, and precipitating events, there is still a possibility that no social movement will emerge, unless there is a mobilization for action in which certain key individuals take the lead (Smelser, 1963). Because it has been suggested that the Internet provided a platform for leaders to move quickly to mobilize the movement (Meador, 1996), the variable called "mobilization for action" was concerned with the type of specific media that the militiamen believed was most helpful in mobilizing the movement. The specific research question that relates to this variable is: Did the Internet play a more important role than other media in helping to mobilize the movement?

### Social Control

Social control, to Smelser (1963), referred to the mechanisms that affected the direction of a movement once it had begun. It is the sum total of mechanisms that disrupt or inhibit a movement in progress, and not social control in the sense of enforcing norms. Here, we are primarily concerned with the electronic implications of the Oklahoma City bombing and specifically, from an electronic standpoint, if social control tactics led to an abandonment of Internet traffic for more secure kinds of communications such as encrypted e-mail messages or the confidential communications within small leaderless cells (Southern

Poverty Law Center, 1996). The related research question is: Following the Oklahoma City bombing, did social control influence movement participants to use the Internet less and "underground" kinds of communications more often? This variable was measured by traffic as recorded in the Usenet archive, *Deja News*.

## Ideological Orientation

An important question left unresolved by the literature review – and an issue unrelated to Smelser's theory - was the issue of the ideological orientation of the neo-militia movement. There was a difference of opinion among writers who stressed the constitutionalism of the militias (Berlet and Lyons, 1995) and those who believed that Christian Identity beliefs underlay most all of the militia rhetoric (Ridgeway and Zeskind, 1995). Therefore, in this study the variable "orientation" was concerned with whether the primary ideology of the militia, or at least that of the individual posting the message, was primarily constitutionalist or primarily Christian Identity. The related research question is: What is the primary orientation of the movement, constitutionalist or Christian Identity?

Messages with constitutionalist content pointed to the New World Order or other generalized belief and the need to train and bear arms to resist a collectivist takeover. Christian Identity messages stressed the militia as an all-Aryan body, upholders of true Israelism, with a very uncompromising stance with respect to religious beliefs, and spoke of a final war against the "forces of darkness" (Aho, 1994), or, nonwhite opponents and their allies.[1]

## Summary

A table in this chapter provides a visual overview of Smelser's theory for those who are not familiar with it. We note that Smelser's preliminary point concerning structural conduciveness is not tested. We believe that the social structure has already been shown to be conducive in that constitutional guarantees allow militias to exist in the first place, and the Internet provided an open forum for militias to organize.

The five major points of Smelser's theory are tested, however. The following research questions were constructed in order to test the theory: 1) Did militiamen/women experience strain prior to or during their tenure in the militia? 2) Before joining the militia, or during militia membership, were militiamen or women introduced to the idea of the New World Order, and did they accept it? 3) Were events at Ruby Ridge and Waco, together with the passage of gun control legislation, important reasons why participants joined the militia? 4) Did the Internet play a more important role than other media in helping to mobilize the movement? 5) Following the Oklahoma City bombing, did social control influence movement participants to use the Internet less and "underground" kinds of communications more often?

An important question left unresolved by the literature review – and an issue unrelated to Smelser's theory – was the issue of the ideological orientation of the neo-militia movement. The opportunity we had to answer this question was too good to pass up, so we decided to seek the answer to the following question: What is the primary orientation of the movement, constitutionalist or Christian Identity?

---

### Note

[1] A note is in order about the limitations of the study. Because this study strives to be for the most part unobtrusive, the data are limited to the examination of recorded communications on the Internet. These communications are mostly the written word or graphics. There is no way to follow up or to probe deeper for a more complete understanding of what any given phrase or sentence meant to the person writing or posting it. Furthermore, there is no way to validate the information published on the Internet by comparing it with questionnaire data or interviews without introducing the problem of respondent reactivity. Militiamen are known for their distrust of academic research and do not interview well (Lindstedt, 1997; Metcalf, 1998). However, to answer the charge that we are not actually getting to know the "real" militia movement through interactive contact, seventeen interviews were conducted with militia members during 2002. A legitimate question could also be raised that this study looks at a socio-economically more affluent subset of the militia movement because it is limited to militiamen who own a computer and have the technological capability to post to the Internet. This suggests a higher level of intelligence and possibly more income than other militiamen. We have already suggested several reasons why this should not be a great concern. However, to attempt to address the possibility of bias this might introduce into the study, in Chapter 8 the results for the 28 "Internet" militias are compared with a group of militiamen who belong to 28 "non-Internet" militias. Informally at least, the non-Internet militias are a control group in the sense that the absence of the Internet is being measured.

# Chapter 6

## Strain, Generalized Beliefs, and Precipitating Events

There was a considerable amount of cross posting of messages to the three Internet newsgroups studied: Miscellaneous-Activism-Militia, Talk-Politics-Guns, and Miscellaneous-Survivalism. Of these three newsgroups, Miscellaneous-Activism-Militia and Talk-Politics-Guns were the most likely groups to be cross-posted, that is, to have an original message posted simultaneously to both groups. Because both groups had high frequencies of daily messages posted, this meant that, when it came time to analyze the data, there was frequent duplication of postings. After eliminating the duplicate postings and upon review and coding of the remaining messages, it was determined that 1,196 messages had sufficient content to be analyzed. One hundred messages were from militia web sites and 1,096 were from militia discussion groups on Usenet.

Structural Strain

Table 5 shows that, indeed, there were multiple strains upon militiamen/women prior to joining the militia or during militia membership. Nine types of strain were identified, the most important of which were indicated by the militiamen as fear of the United States federal government. Over 63 percent of the messages related to the first question expressed this fear of the government. Within this 63 percent, 30 percent feared that federal and/or international police forces were growing in power; 20 percent mentioned a fear of government without elaborating in more detail; and 13 percent felt that the federal government with its harsh and repressive policies was becoming more like the former Soviet Union. A militiaman (post 12) who was fearful of the growing power of U.S. federal police posted this message about this particular strain:

> Experts who have been watching such developments say all this is leading one place - to the establishment of a genuine national police force. You can see it in the way the FBI now routinely interferes in local law enforcement affairs. You can also see it in the plans of big-government architects... who [have] urged that Treasury Department police agencies... be placed under the control of the Justice Department.

Another militiaman, fearing the "Sovietization" of U.S. police forces, expressed the following: "I am scared that we are becoming a police state a la Nazi Germany or Stalinist Russia. I do not want to be slave labor" (post 238).

The remaining 37 percent of the responses were as follows: 8 percent indicated that they experienced economic distress; 6 percent had experienced rapid social changes; 6 percent said that their standard of living was declining; 6 percent said that globalization had affected them, or that they had lost their jobs; 6 percent indicated a distrust of government or a discontent with it; and 5 percent listed strains other than those mentioned above.

The fear of the federal government that we found in this study has also been documented by other researchers who, like Smelser, agree that is a precondition for the growth of the neo militia movement (Karl 1995; Kushner 1998). As militiamen in this study described it, this fear centers on the unchecked growth and power of the federal government

**Table 5**
**Structural Strain Reported by/for U.S. Militiamen/Women**

| Reported Strain | Number | Percent |
| --- | --- | --- |
| Fear federal/global police force | 38 | 30.4 |
| Fear federal government | 25 | 20.0 |
| Fear U.S. "Soviet" state | 16 | 12.8 |
| Economic distress (unspecified) | 10 | 8.0 |
| Rapid social change | 8 | 6.4 |
| Shrinking standard of living | 8 | 6.4 |
| Globalization or job loss | 7 | 5.6 |
| Distrust of or discontent with government | 7 | 5.6 |
| Other | 6 | 4.8 |
| Total | 125 | 100.0 |

and its tendency to develop a federal policing model that resembles that of the former Soviet Union. Bennett (1995) came across both kinds of fear as he interviewed citizen militiamen. In fact, Bennett referred to the militias as "the new party of fear," with fear playing so prominently a role as to be the organizing theme of this new movement (p. 446). He quotes a Missouri Militia license plate he believes reflects the concerns of many militiamen: "I love my country but I fear my government." He continues with a quotation from Norm Olson of the Michigan Militia: "it is not anger we feel, it is fear, fear of the federal government" (p. xi.). Elaborating upon the source of this fear, Olson said: "it's not a Government by the people anymore... we are ceasing to be a Republic. The people's fear is a response. When people sense danger, they will come together to defend themselves" (p. 456).

The fear militiamen feel can be total, affecting their whole lives. As Harold Sheil of the 51$^{st}$ Missouri Militia noted: "One of the things that people really fear from the government is the idea that the government can ruin your life, totally destroy your life. I don't mean kill you. But they can totally destroy your life, split your family up, do the whole thing and walk off like you're a discarded banana peel, and with a ho-hum attitude" (Snow, 1999: 27).

There was also fear expressed in some of the messages in this study that the United States was becoming more repressive and totalitarian, modeling itself after the former Soviet Union. Bennett (1995) notes this concern as well among militiamen he studied. If the Russian menace was no longer there, and there was genuine peace in the world, why was it that a huge, centralized federal bureaucracy was still needed?

McAlvaney (1990), who operates a Patriot research service, wrote an entire book on this theme. The basic idea of the book was that the Russian "Bear" lives on, that it has conquered the United Nations and the New World Order, and that it is still bent on worldwide domination and the establishment of a worldwide socialist government. By aiding this menace and not challenging it, the U.S. is lending tacit approval to the Soviet takeover and is acceding to Russian methods of social control. John Trochmann of the Militia of Montana spoke of this idea in his visit and speech at Yale University (Cheong, 1995).

If the fears articulated in this study are somehow different from those documented elsewhere, it is because militiamen here seemed reluctant to mention specific issues of a personal nature that other militiamen had mentioned to other researchers, for instance, the fear that government agents and/or police will interfere in private family matters (divorce, custody battles), may over regulate their businesses resulting in financial ruin, may confiscate weapons, or may take away freedom of religion.

The results in Table 5 show only a residual concern about jobs and/or economics. Only 20 percent of the messages indicated a concern with economic distress, declining standard of living or globalization. In general, then, the strains mentioned by the militiamen or women were not job related. There was very little evidence to suggest that the militiamen were displaced workers and that the displacements were due to global economic restructuring.

In fact, occupational data in Table 6 show that 53 percent of the militiamen for whom data were available could be classified as professional and managerial; 17 percent as sales, technical, or administrative; 22 percent as manual labor; and 8 percent as low skill or service. Comparisons in the table with the U.S. population as a whole indicate that militiamen are overrepresented among the professional and managerial group and underrepresented among the other groups when compared with the general population of the United States. Thus, the occupational data, albeit based upon a limited number of cases, do not suggest economic marginality or that the militiamen are under any particular economic strain due to their current occupations.

A cautionary note is warranted given the low response rate to this particular question. The data may be reflecting the "pride" of the employed militia members and the "embarrassment" of those not employed or underemployed. It is impossible to measure this given that probe questions cannot be asked.

Similarly, other research confirms that militia membership crosses class lines. An anthropology doctoral student who joined a Florida militia later wrote how the militia was a mixture of "solid citizens" and a few that were marginal. He wrote that membership cut across traditional class boundaries and included business owners, corporate executives, lawyers and doctors intermingled with "rednecks," the unemployed and menial labor (Keen, 1998; see also Snow, 1999 and Kushner, 1998).

**Table 6**
**Occupations Reported by/for U.S. Militiamen/Women***

| Reported Occupations | Number | Percent | Percent As Compared with U.S. Population* |
|---|---|---|---|
| Professional/Managerial | 18 | 52.5 | 27.0 |
| Sales/Technical/Admin** | 20 | 17.0 | 31.0 |
| Manual Labor | 13 | 22.0 | 25.0 |
| Low Skill/Service Sector | 3 | 8.5 | 17.0 |
| Total | 54 | 100.0 | 100.0 |

Notes:    *Source: U.S. Census (1994).
**These figures include reports by/for militiamen of "middle class" social standing without further elaboration. See Appendix D.

**Table 7**
**Militiamen/Women Accepting Concept of New World Order**
**(before or during Militia Membership)**

|  | Number | Percent |
|---|---|---|
| Accepted NWO Concept | 57 | 51.8 |
| Did Not Accept NWO Concept (rejected NWO or accepted an alternative belief such as ZOG or police state) | 53 | 48.2 |
| Total | 110 | 100.00 |

Notes:    Data are not available for 61 of the militiamen or women.
           Militiamen/women reporting = 110. Relevant messages = 110.


Generalized Beliefs


Table 7 corresponds to the second research question: Before joining the militia, or during militia membership, were militiamen or women introduced to the idea of the New World Order, and did they accept it? The data indicate that there was no significant difference in the number of militiamen who accepted or did not accept the concept of the New World Order prior to or during their membership in the militia. Case number 42, a strong advocate for the idea of the New World Order, said that militia wrath is centered on the United Nations because it is controlled by an alliance between big business and the Soviet Union, who are intent upon destroying America and creating a New World Order (post 104). Like many others, this person clearly accepted the notion of the NWO.

Interestingly, over 48 percent of the militiamen for whom information was available reported that they had not been introduced to the New World Order prior to joining the militia, or during militia membership or, if introduced to the idea, did not accept it. Some had become familiar instead with the Zionist Occupational Government or ZOG. This is similar to the New World Order idea. ZOG is Jewish-controlled U.S. federal government that is trying to impose a one-world socialist government. A communiqué from the Aryan Republican Army (post 250), a group in opposition to ZOG, stated:

> We call ourselves the Aryan Republican Army because in
> some of our tactics, and some of our goals, we have
> modeled the organization after the successful and yet
> undefeated Irish Republican Army... The Irish, another
> tribe of the Aryan people, have fought off the Jewish-
> inspired elite of the English.

An observer of the ARA noted: "It [the ARA] is committed to the
overthrow of the U.S. government, the extermination of America's
Jews, and the establishment of an "Aryan Republic" on the North
American continent" (post 284).

Another alternative could be called "police state." This idea is
basically that law enforcement at all levels is abusive, corrupt, and
exercising executive powers well beyond its mandate. As one advocate
(post 297) put it:

> I was... outraged when government forces firebombed an
> inner city neighborhood of Philadelphia in 1985, killing
> 11... and then there are the countless murders and cover-ups
> by "law enforcement" that have become common-place in
> my community.

Other militiamen simply did not accept the idea of the NWO and
clearly did not think it was important. Two of the militiamen (posts 111
and 238) responded:

> "New World Order" is probably not the term used by the
> shadow government to refer to their strategic plan. It
> appears to have been invented by conspiracy theorists, and
> its use detracts from our credibility.

> We do not think about the NWO; this is an urban myth
> perpetuated by the media.

Yet another example of a militia completely unconcerned with the New
World Order is the Cascade (Washington) Brigade. This group works
openly with law enforcement and within the political system to bring
about changes in government. It is anti-government in the sense that it
believes the government is too large and should be reduced in size and
scope. Cascade's leader, case number 48, knew of the NWO but did not
think that it was an important concept. He (post 298) states:

> [The New World Order and other issues] are valid concerns by various individuals, but for the most part, I think that most are mainly concerned with getting the Federal Government down to a manageable and constitutionally relative size. Most are folks that want to be able to talk to the people that have control over the things that concern their daily lives, without having to buy a ticket to Washington DC and stomping through the bureaucratic halls of a bloated and convoluted government where no one seems accountable for anything.

After data collection, a further review of relevant literature did reveal the existence of competing generalized beliefs (e.g., ZOG, police state) and evidence that some militiamen/women simply did not believe in the New World Order (Karl, 1995; Hoffman, 1995; Stern, 1995; Macko, 1996; Snow, 1999). For example, researchers have reported that the militiamen who joined Christian Identity oriented militias were more likely to have been introduced to skinhead culture – and ZOG - first, and sometime after that, to Christian Identity beliefs (e.g., Macko, 1996).

Moreover, the literature showed that the "police state" generalized belief had grown in popularity, so much so that it is being touted as the primary alternative to the idea of the New World Order. *The Resister*, a publication of the Special Forces Underground, states the vision thusly: "The increasing militarization of federal, state and local law enforcement agencies, aided by the duplicity of the Department of Defense has created the very beast feared by the founders generally and the antifederalists specifically; an armed force under the exclusive control of the executive branch of the federal government. These federal agencies have no purpose other than the enforcement of arbitrary, undefined, whim-based federal 'laws'" (Stern, 1995: 158).

Smelser did not specify that one and only one generalized belief occurred with the onset of each new social movement. More than one could be present, and he referred to five different types. One of these, the hostile belief, is salient to the neo militias. It is salient not only to the New World Order but also to the other generalized beliefs uncovered in the study. The hostile belief identifies the source of strain, seeks to mobilize to attack this agent, and exaggerates the power to remove the source of evil. Hence, in the case of the NWO or ZOG, it is this "evil beast" that is the source and the force driving the involvement of U.S. governmental agents into the private lives of American citizens.

It, the beast, is the source of America's slide into collectivism, rather than the government or its agents per se. This allows many militiamen and women to remain true U.S. patriots, committed to the U.S. Constitution without being anti-American. According to Smelser, mobilization of arms to protect citizens from attack becomes the suggested means of coping with this agent, and there is "wishful thinking" that these mobilized groups can actually gather up the power to remove the source of evil.


Precipitating Events


The third research question asked if events at Ruby Ridge and Waco together with gun control legislation were the most important precipitating events that prompted individuals to join militias or to remain in them. According to Table 8, Waco and Ruby Ridge were the most frequently mentioned precipitants of the U.S. neo militia movement. These two events were mentioned by 77 percent of the individuals posting a message relevant to this research question. On the other hand, the Brady Bill was mentioned in only 11 percent of the messages and the Assault Weapons Bill of 1994 was mentioned in only 6 percent of the messages. A 1992 meeting at Estes Park, Colorado, believed by some writers to be an important catalyst of the militia movement, was mentioned in only 2 percent of the relevant messages.


**Table 8**
**Precipitants of U.S. Militia Movement Mentioned**
**by/for U.S. Militiamen/Women**

| Event | Number | Percent |
|---|---|---|
| Waco | 136 | 40.6 |
| Ruby Ridge | 121 | 36.1 |
| Brady Bill | 38 | 11.3 |
| Assault Weapons Bill | 20 | 6.0 |
| Estes Park meeting | 7 | 2.1 |
| Other (LA Riot, MOVE, Desert Storm) | 7 | 2.1 |
| G.H.W. Bush's NWO Speech (1990) | 6 | 1.8 |
| Total | 335 | 100.0 |

There is substantial corroborating documentation that these two events are the primary precipitants of the movement (Barkun, 1995; Karl, 1995; Walter, 1995; Halpern and Levin, 1996; Hamm, 1997; Kushner, 1998; Snow, 1999). The future militiamen and women--those studied here as well as those in other studies--wondered why so much federal firepower was allocated for Weaver, living in a dilapidated shed in an isolated part of Idaho with his wife and family, and for the Branch Davidians, a small and unpopular religious sect. These militia individuals were deeply troubled by the raw force that led to loss of life at Ruby Ridge and Waco (Koernke, 1993; Thompson, 1993; Bennett, 1995).

These two events therefore became powerful symbols of an out-of-control federal government, that was intent on NWO or ZOG, and that would stop at nothing to impose its will upon helpless citizens. Extremist watchers promoted the idea that weapons legislation was an important precipitant, but the data in this study did not support this contention. The brute force exercised at Waco and Ruby Ridge confirmed the generalized beliefs in a more complete way than any group of weapons bills could possibly confirm. Books and especially videos about the two events circulated quickly among those who were instrumental in forming militias and among those who would join later (Koernke, 1993, 1994; Thompson, 1993, 1994).

## Summary

The first three of the major points in Smelser's theory of collective behavior have been generally confirmed by the data collected in our study so far. A majority of militia persons reported enduring some kind of social strain prior to or during their stay in the citizen militia. This strain was most commonly described as a fear of the power of the U.S. federal government. In an unexpected finding, militia people reported more than one generalized belief being important to them prior to or during militia membership. As we discussed, Smelser's theory did not specify that one and only one generalized belief would arise to provide an explanation for social strain. More than one belief could emerge, and that was what we found in this study. Events at Ruby Ridge and Waco were most often cited as key precipitants for people who joined the militia, and the show of federal force in these events proved more powerful overall than the concerns about gun control.

Chapter 7

# Mobilization, Social Control, and Ideological Orientations of the Militia Movement

## Mobilization for Action

To answer the fourth research question concerning the importance of the Internet in helping to mobilize the movement (see Table 9), 48 percent of the messages indicate Internet, Usenet, or computer bulletin boards as the preferred media compared with only 21 percent that preferred faxes. Though a number of other media were mentioned less frequently (shortwave radio, talk shows, cable TV, videos, e-mail, direct mail), messages stressed that the media were not in competition with one another but were, when taken as a whole, a credible alternative source of information and much preferred overall to the mainstream media.

**Table 9**
**Media of Choice Reported by/for U.S. Militiamen/Women**

| Media | Number | Percent |
|---|---|---|
| Bulletin boards/Usenet/Internet | 71 | 48.0 |
| FAX | 31 | 20.9 |
| Short wave radio | 17 | 11.5 |
| Talk shows/cable TV/videos | 11 | 7.4 |
| E-mail | 9 | 6.1 |
| Direct mail | 9 | 6.1 |
| Total | 148 | 100.0 |

Smelser's theory emphasizes the key role of leaders in mobilizing a movement such as a militia movement. Table 10 indicates how key mentors with the technological skill to master the Internet played a largely successful role during a crucial phase of movement mobilization from early 1993 to the first anniversary of the end of the Waco massacre of April 19, 1994. This mobilization of the Internet was of extreme importance in that, to both militia mentors and "mentees," the mainstream media had shown that it was not credible, especially after what they considered the "misinformation" and distorted coverage of the movement following the Oklahoma City bombing.

Several researchers note that the movement leaders benefited from trends in technology that existed at the end of the Waco standoff and thus grasped an historic opportunity to act. By the time of the birth of the movement in 1994, computers and computer services were cheaper, quicker, and more readily available than ever before. The Internet newsgroups allowed speedy transmission to a huge audience, including remote rural states. Anyone with access to Usenet (obtainable through CompuServe, America Online, or other providers) could easily subscribe to these groups. This easy access made it possible for certain key documents to be available to the movement quickly and early on in the movement, e.g. the *Texas Militia Papers* and the Michigan Militia manual that was published on Linda Thompson's bulletin board in early 1994 (Parfrey and Redden, 1994; Karl, 1995; Snow, 1999). The Internet mentors use of such technology was masterful; and the importance of the Internet itself to the movement cannot be underestimated. Meador (1996) simply called it "the platform" for the militia movement.

**Table 10**
**Internet Mentors of the U.S. Militia Movement**

| Mentor | Internet Contribution |
| --- | --- |
| Jon Roland, Texas Constitutional Militia | Authored Texas Militia Papers; webmaster of the Constitution Society page |
| Bob Fletcher, Militia of Montana | Webmaster of the Militia of Montana web site |
| Bo Gritz | Personal web page featured information on paramilitary training courses |
| J.J. Johnson | Major contributor to *E Pluribus Unum*, web site affiliated with Ohio Unorganized Militia |
| Martin Lindstedt, 7th Missouri Militia | Editor and Publisher of the Internet magazine, *Modern Militiaman* |
| Linda Thompson | Her BBS was one of the first Patriot bulletin boards; published the Michigan Militia manual in 1994 |

Social Control

Results of Table 11 (corresponding to question five) show that Usenet, a public form of communication, was used with increasing frequency after the Oklahoma City bombing. Smelser's theory suggested that forcing a movement "underground" was one of the possible outcomes of social control, and the literature review suggests that many groups had gone underground. Thus, there was a reasonable expectation that Usenet traffic might decline over time. Instead, the number of messages posted to three militia-oriented news groups by or about the 171

**Table 11**
**Growth in Usenet Traffic on Three Militia-Oriented News Groups**
**(Militia Traffic Only)**

| News Group | Number of Messages Posted from | | |
| --- | --- | --- | --- |
| | Apr. 20, 1995 to Dec. 31, 1996 | Jan. 1, 1997 to Sep. 11, 1998 | Percent Increase or Decrease |
| Miscellaneous-Activism-Militia | 1,444 | 2,864 | +98 |
| Talk-Politics-Guns[a] | 542 | 596 | +10 |
| Miscellaneous-Survivalism | 200 | 135 | -33 |
| Total | 2,186 | 3,595 | +64 |

Notes:  This is traffic by or about the 28 militias studied here; this is the "militia traffic" only.

[a] Using the <u>Deja News</u> power search function, the archive was checked for messages that included the term "militia." Only those messages that had content relevant to the militias were reviewed. This procedure effectively screened out messages that were not militia-related.

militiamen increased from 2,186 during a twenty-month period immediately after the bombing, to 3,595 in a comparable period in 1997-1998, a 64 percent increase. This occurred despite evidence in eighty messages that many militias went underground after the bombing and engaged in more secure kinds of communications: computer bulletin boards, encrypted e-mail, heavily coded messages, and the confidential talk of leaderless cells.

The growth in militia traffic on the Internet following the Oklahoma City bombing has been noted elsewhere in the research literature (cf., Southern Poverty Law Center, 1996). This trend would appear to support the view that militia membership grew after and in spite of the bombing.

However, John George and Laird Wilcox (1996) offer the opposite view. They contend that many militiamen and women dropped out after the bombing (due to the FBI hotline on tips to the bombing) and as mentioned earlier, our messages confirm this. Given these conflicting interpretations, the growth in Internet traffic deserves careful study.

How can we account for the growth in this traffic, especially at a time when there is evidence that militia membership was declining? A number of explanations are feasible.

First, we know that Internet traffic grew because militiamen utilized Usenet as an acceptable alternative media that was relatively free from censoring. This medium was used early and often as movement participants closed ranks to defend themselves in the early post Oklahoma City period.

Second, a number of militia controversies were reported in the mainstream press; later, a militia-approved "correct" interpretation and coverage appeared in the mostly unfiltered Usenet messages (cf., Kemp, 1998.) For example, the Alabama militias' infiltration of a BATF party in Tennessee, the search for John Doe II (unnamed suspect in the Oklahoma City bombing) including the prolific electronic magazine <u>John Doe Times</u>, the arrest of several militia leaders during 1996, and the "show trials" the following year were all given their "proper explanation" and interpretation on the Internet. Militiamen preferred the unfiltered Internet version of events, citing the mainstream press as unfair and unreliable.

Third, by 1996 the movement was beginning to splinter, which contributed to the traffic by adding controversial topics for discussion as well as longer discussion threads. For example, case 83 broke from the constitutionalists and joined the Christian Identity faction. He engaged in some long and bitter threads with his former constitutionalist peers. Then, a common law faction and an anti militia faction (including ex-militiamen) engaged in some bitter debates with both constitutionalists and Christian Identity. These exchanges periodically spilled over into discussions of current events such as the Littleton, Colorado school shootings and the war in Kosovo, with the warring parties invariably taking opposite sides. Some militiamen or militia sympathizers went on to produce electronic magazines that, when posted in their entirety, were typically several times longer than even the longest of individual postings by or about individual militiamen. Such discussions added to the increase in traffic in the militia-oriented newsgroups.

Fourth, some militias continued to use the Internet even after officially closing up shop and going underground. For example, the 7th Missouri Militia told interested persons or newcomers to form private leaderless cells, while at the same time, it continued to publish its web site as a political education tool and its leader continued to post prolifically to the Miscellaneous-Activism-Militia category. In this particular leader's view of things, web sites and Usenet postings function as political education and propaganda while the leaderless cells serve as the "action arm" of the organization.

Is it possible that the increase on the three discussion groups is simply a reflection of an overall increased interest in the Internet as a means of communication? To test this idea we would need to look at the total traffic on several different types of newsgroups during the two time frames we are studying. Ideally we would have compared the traffic on the three militia-oriented groups with three mainstream discussion groups, for example, those of the Democratic, Republican, and Reform parties. Due to the demise of the superior search engine <u>Deja News</u> in February, 2001, such accurate comparisons are unfortunately no longer possible.

However, we can compare the numbers of "militia" postings on the three news groups studied with the total traffic on those newsgroups. As Table 12 shows, the overall traffic, which included militia and nonmilitia messages, increased in all three news groups by 111 percent overall. Perhaps unexpectedly, we found that the militia postings were only about 3 to 4 percent of the total postings, if we compare the results of Table 11 with Table 12. This indicates that a huge percentage of posters to the militia-oriented news groups covers a wide rage of people who have some interest in militias but a very large contingent who do not belong to any militia. Hence, overall, the posters ranged from people with a casual curiosity about militias, to militia "wannabes," to serious and active militia members who were having event-focused, specific dialogues with one another. The "nonmilitia" traffic, which we perused occasionally, reflected great diversity: it consisted of (among others) (1) "reluctant" posters who were sympathetic but could not join a militia for some reason, (2) derogatory, flaming messages critical of militias in general, or (3) cross-talk, that is, messages that were simply cross-posted to several news groups at once. The fact that militia traffic is so small and did not increase as fast suggests that more factors may be at work than simply the overall increase in volume. In any event, we cannot conclude that the increase in militia traffic was simply "riding the coattails" of a general increased interest in the Internet.

**Table 12**
**Growth in Usenet Traffic on Three Militia-Oriented News Groups**
**(Militia and Non-Militia Traffic)**

| | Number of Messages Posted from | | |
| --- | --- | --- | --- |
| News Group | Apr. 20, 1995 to Dec. 31, 1996 | Jan. 1, 1997 to Sep. 11, 1998 | Percent Increase or Decrease |
| Miscellaneous-Activism-Militia | 41,811 | 81,978 | +96 |
| Talk-Politics-Guns[a] | 7,642 | 23,027 | +201 |
| Miscellaneous-Survivalism | 808 | 1,174 | +45 |
| Total | 50,261 | 106,179 | +111 |

Notes:  This is <u>all</u> the traffic in the newsgroup, both militia and non-militia.
[a] Using the <u>Deja News</u> power search function, the archive was checked for messages that included the term "militia." Only those messages that had content relevant to the militias were reviewed. This procedure effectively screened out messages that were not militia-related.

Smelser believed that social control would influence the direction of a movement once it starts. The neo militia movement is one example of this phenomenon, at least according to the messages studied. Social control drove some militias underground, as eighty messages suggested, but apparently not completely out of the public domain. They were still able to reach and influence other militiamen or potential militia recruits via the Internet and to argue their case against their antagonists. Thus, while social control played a role in the direction of the movement, that specific direction was not the one suggested by the bulk of the literature review. Most of the reviewed literature suggested that militias would go underground and "drop out," abandoning public forums such as the Internet. Social control also led to the adoption of tactics that could not easily have been predicted as the movement began. Several messages suggested that "leaderless resistance" (Beam,

1992) in small self-contained cells is the model of a militia that goes underground. This redirection of the movement, with an emphasis upon impenetrability, is also something that Smelser's theory suggests.

The content of specific messages show an interesting, distinct change in the ways the militias studied employed Usenet as one compares the content of messages in time frames 1 and 2. In the first time frame, Usenet was utilized mostly to exchange information, to build consensus and to generally render aid and assistance to fellow militiamen, most of whom were under attack for their alleged participation in (or encouragement of) the Oklahoma City bombing. For example, post 18 from case number 83 in 1996 illustrates an amicable tone:

> In May 1996 I went with some fellow Missourians to Gadsden, Alabama for a militia rally called the Good 'Ol Boys Roundup... It was an excellent militia gathering. People who I had formerly known only by means of e-mail I met in person and vice-versa. They are good people who will find themselves having to do hard things in the future, if they are to hold true to their vision of freedom and justice under a government limited by law.

By 1997, following a very difficult year in which federal agents infiltrated several militias and incriminating evidence was presented in a series of militia "show trials," bitter divisions were developing within the movement. The constitutionalists separated themselves ideologically from the Christian Identity faction. In turn, individuals posting messages from Posse Comitatus and the Common Law movement criticized both the constitutionalists and the Christian Identity faction. Throughout 1997 and most of 1998, there were angry, personal exchanges between individuals in all four of these camps. For example, this 1998 message from case 83 to a former ally notes: "I point out that if you hate us so much, you simply have no right to live as a parasite off of us and among us. We neither want nor need to have you around. Go live among those you serve. Practice what you preach" (post 78). Case 83 had shorn his early constitutionalism for Christian Identity.

Finally, there were anti-Patriot and anti-militia posters joining the fray who were critical of most everything discussed in the groups by all parties in all discussions. All of this new participation no doubt contributed to the rise in the number of postings reflected in Tables 11-12. From 1997 through most of 1998, this pattern continued, as Usenet was employed by militias less for information exchange and more as a forum to comment on current events and/or to expound on the differences between different factions posting to the newsgroups.


Ideological Orientation


Data in Table 13, corresponding to the sixth research question, reveal that 65 percent of the relevant messages indicated that the purpose of the militia is to further constitutionalist aims, while 35 percent indicated that the militia's purpose is to further Christian Identity goals. Individual militiamen who composed messages portraying a Constitutionalist orientation often went out of their way to separate themselves ideologically from Christian Identity militiamen, and vice versa. A militiaman (post 31) whose message was representative of the constitutionalist orientation is as follows:

> ...the bulk of the... militias of the various United States have formed a grass roots response to... government-sponsored terrorism as well as the continued degradation of our constitutional rights at the hands of the current federal administration.

A Christian Identity militiaman posted this incendiary message for his former constitutionalist allies to read: "Frankly [you Constitutionalists] hate White People. You really hate those of us fighting to restore White America for White People" (post 78).


**Table 13**
**Ideological Orientations Reported by/for U.S.
Militiamen/Women**

| Primary Orientation | | Number | Percent |
|---|---|---|---|
| Constitutionalist | | 345 | 65 |
| Christian Identity | | 186 | 35 |
| | Total | 531 | 100 |


Other researchers have confirmed what appears to be the constitutionalist bent of the current movement (Bennett, 1995; Kushner, 1998). In the current study, about two-thirds of the messages posted related to the question about ideology indicated content supportive of constitutionalism. The remaining one-third had content indicative of Christian Identity. While it is difficult to make the bold statement that most militia men and women are constitutionalists based on a limited number of Internet messages, the two-to-one ratio in the messages mirrors those estimates made by extremist watchers and even some militiamen concerning the actual proportion of movement members who are constitutionalists or Christian Identity (Stern, 1996; Lindstedt, 1998).

While all orientations could be generally classified as Christian Identity or constitutionalist, and in many cases the coding of the messages was unambiguous, the messages did suggest (upon further analysis) a rich variety in the orientations of the militias, consequently it was appropriate to designate a typology of militia organizations. This typology is presented in Table 14, along with a listing of representative militias.

Type 1 is the open constitutionalist militias that work freely with law enforcement and are completely open to all who want to participate. The anti-government rhetoric of this type of militia resembles that of mainstream conservatives. Washington's Cascade Brigade is an example of this type. Completely open to public scrutiny, their agenda is not much different from any other mainstream conservative interest group.

Type 2 is the open constitutionalist militias with a command structure. Here, there are small regiments usually organized at the county level and have a hierarchical military style command structure. For the most part, their operations are conducted publicly. The Michigan Militia Corps serves as an example.

Type 3 is the constitutionalist militia/survivalist/cell structure type, with a correspondence structure. Here, there are small regiments usually organized at the county level. Constitutionalist goals and philosophy are expounded, but survivalism is the encouraged or preferred lifestyle, along with the formation of leaderless cells. Publicly identified commanders may serve as information sources for regiments/cells. These commanders may be the only source of contact that the cell has with the outside world. The Texas Constitutional Militia is probably the purest example of this type.

Type 4 is the militia that is completely underground and has ceased almost all contact with the public. We may only learn of their existence if a member is convicted of a crime, or if the group signs a public declaration such as the Alabama Declaration that was published to the

Internet in 1996. Alabama's Sons of Liberty are an example: they signed the declaration but beyond that, their operations have been secret.


**Table 14**
**A Typology of Six Militia Organizational Models**
**with Corresponding Examples of Representative Militias**

| Model | Ideological Orientation | Organizational Examples |
|---|---|---|
| Open Constitutionalist | Constitutionalist | Cascade Brigade |
| Constitutionalist/Command Structure | Constitutionalist | Alabama Constitutional Militia<br>Michigan Militia |
| Constitutionalist/Cell Structure | Constitutionalist | Militia of Montana<br><br>Texas Constitutional Militia |
| Underground/No Public Contact: | Constitutionalist | Sons of Liberty (Alabama) |
| Terrorism/Irish Republican Army | Christian Identity | Aryan Republican Army |
| Sinn Fein/Irish Republican Army: | Christian Identity | 7th Missouri Militia<br><br>91st Brigade |

Type 5 is the Terrorist/Irish Republican Army Model of terrorist cells without an organized political wing. Here the production of propaganda is a part time pursuit of members of cells. The group models itself after the IRA but is left to form its own propaganda in the form of a series of communiqués issued after missions are complete. The Aryan Republican Army, a group that committed a number of bank robberies in the Midwest to raise funds, is an example of this type. They occasionally issued public communiqués after their robberies, but there was no formal political wing established.

Type 6 is the Sinn Fein/Irish Republican Army Model, where there is a political education wing and terrorist leaderless cells that are the action arm. For example, as individuals approach the 7th Missouri Militia about joining, they are encouraged to form leaderless cells and then to rely upon the militia's substantial Internet resources if needed for guidance, support or a rationalization for a mission. The militia's web site also is, in general, a political action wing, fulfilling some of the functions of the Sinn Fein in Northern Ireland.

It should be pointed out that the militias cited as examples above are the purest representation that we could find of each type. In reality, many militias are a hybrid of several types illustrated above. The literature on militias appears to confirm the diversity that we found in terms of different types of militia groups. Scholars have acknowledged that the movement is difficult to classify largely because of this diversity (Kushner, 1998). Meador (1996) noted a "citizen activist" worldview among militiamen that was similar to those who joined the open constitutionalist militias that were examined in this study (e.g. Cascade Brigade). She also encountered an "enforcer" or protector type whose profile resembles the militiamen in the open constitutionalist militias that had a command structure such as the Michigan Militia and the Alabama Constitutional Militia. Finally, she notes a "separatist" world view similar to that voiced by militiamen who joined the survivalist/cell structure militias such as the Militia of Montana and the Texas Constitutional Militia. These militiamen are the kind that stockpile food and weapons, fearing a civil war between U.S. government agents and militias.

Over 100 militiamen/women were contacted via email for interviews during the first quarter of 2002. Seventeen persons eventually responded to six research questions that asked questions parallel to the questions in this study that have already been discussed in the last two chapters. This was done in part to see if the information discovered in interviews might be different than that captured on the Internet. In a way, this is a "validation test" for the Internet data.

Based on the interviews completed, it does not appear that there were any significant differences between the interview respondents and those who posted to the Internet. The interviewees in general indicated a fear of government that provided a backdrop for their joining a militia. These quotes are quite similar to ones that appeared in Chapter 6: "(I am) more fearful of the government within than the peoples outside the U.S... the corolaries (sic) between pre-Nazi Germany and the current political climate in America scared the Hell out of me (Interview 2).

If the interviews were different in any way from the textual "message" data cited in chapter 6, it would be that, in the context of an interview, the militiapersons seemed more comfortable expressing a specific fear of what government might do to restrict their freedoms; gun control was frequently mentioned. (This finding mirrors that of Bennett [1995] who found a wide variety of very specific fears that were of concern to the militiamen with whom he spoke.) This willingness to speak frankly and personally about the fears was noticeably absent in the Internet postings.

There was a difference of opinion (that was much like what we found in the Internet postings) about the New World Order: some said that it existed and they clearly accepted it while others downplayed the idea. Consider the differences between these two interviewees (Interviews 5 and 14, respectively):

> The New World Order has nothing whatsoever to do with a
> constitutional militia.

> It would amaze me that any American with the power to
> think does NOT believe that the New World Order exists.

Waco was mentioned as an important precipitant, and was mentioned more than Ruby Ridge. This was exactly what we found earlier. The interviewees were avid Internet users and have continued to use the Internet, even in the post-Oklahoma City spotlight that militia members have been under.

Finally, most of those interviewed viewed themselves as Constitutionalists. Christian Identity believers appeared to be underrepresented among the interviewees.

It is significant to note that several interviewees indicated an advanced knowledge of computer technology and said that their friends in the militia had similar skills. In the interviews it was common to hear the something along these lines: "For my part, I am a computer professional, as are many militia activists" (Interview 6). "Prior to formally swearing in as a member of my particular group, I was a somewhat conservative computer professional" (Interview 14).

This is important in the whole issue of whether a group of Internet messages posted by militia people actually represents the movement as a whole. An argument could possibly be made that most of the movement is not plugged in to the computer; thus, studying Internet postings gives a skewed picture of the overall movement. The Internet postings would only be by the "upper class" of the movement that owns computers and knows how to use them. The results of the interviews suggested that militia people had been plugged in for years, even before the average American consumer, and adapting to the Internet as a medium of communication was not difficult at all. That is what we had argued earlier, based largely on the work of Chip Berlet and others who had studied the electronic aspects of the movement in detail. The interviews appear to confirm our argument. Several interviewees spoke of their years of experience with computers and computer technology.


## Summary


This chapter examined the last two major points in Smelser's theory as well as the issue of the ideological orientations of the militiamen and women, an issue that was not satisfactorily resolved in the literature review.

The Internet was mentioned most often as the media of choice for militia people. This makes sense as scholars had pointed out the importance of the Internet in mobilizing the movement. Smelser believed that social control agents play a role in the direction taken by a movement, and the militia movement is no exception. The expectation was that social control would lead to less Internet use. The findings in the chapter were to the contrary. Despite federal intervention in militia affairs, in which it is known that many militias did subsequently go underground, the traffic on the Internet did not decrease, for a number of practical reasons enumerated in the chapter. The primary ideological orientation of the militia groups studied appears to be constitutionalism, however, it is important to point out that this conclusion is based upon a relatively small number of Internet messages examined.

Interviews conducted with militia people during 2002 mostly validated the Internet data collected in the last chapter and in this one.

Many reported social stress in the form of fear of the federal government – results very similar to those reported in earlier chapters. The interviewees were more likely to reveal personal fears than those who posted messages. Also paralleling the finding of earlier chapters, there was a disagreement about the New World Order: some believed in it while others did not. Waco was the most frequently mentioned precipitant, and most interviewees identified themselves as Constitutionalists. Importantly, many claimed to have long standing computer experience. This was an important piece in determining the overall representativeness of the sample of the 171 militia people that we studied.

Chapter 8

# Internet and Non-Internet-Based Militias: A Comparison

In Chapter 4 of this book, several questions were raised about the representativeness of the sample of militias that were selected for study. Of particular concern was the fact that all the militia people studied were Internet users, or at least the leadership of the militia had such skills. Thus, a question to be raised is, does our study look at a socio-economically more affluent subset of the militia movement because it is limited to militiamen and women who own a computer and have the technological capability to post to the Internet? This would suggest a higher level of intelligence and possibly more income than other militiamen or women. Corollary questions could also be asked: are the message posters truly representative of a broader group of militia members who may or may not use the Internet? Is the Internet user group a unique subset of all militia members, a distinctive set of leaders, or more typical of the "average" militia member?

The answer to these questions raised in Chapter 4 is that there was a large group of patriots in the 1980s that had been plugged in to computer bulletin board systems (BBS) for many years prior to the appearance of the Internet. When the Internet arrived, they were already sophisticated computer users, or at very least had a basic understanding that allowed them to function in a computer bulletin board environment. The transition from BBS to Internet was easy; so easy that even the average militia person was able to access the Internet and its network of discussion groups called Usenet.

We now accept the fact that some sociologists would be unconvinced of the representativeness of the sample, even after the explanation given above. In the final analysis, perhaps the only way to address the issue of representativeness is to study a group of militia people who do not have an Internet web address, or whose militia did not qualify as having a significant amount of traffic in the Usenet discussion groups.

This is the purpose of this chapter. We study non-Internet-based militias along the dimensions suggested by Smelser's theory, i.e., strain, generalized beliefs, precipitating events, mobilization for action, and social control. We also look at the ideological orientation of these militias. Then, this information will be compared with what we have learned about the "Internet" militias in Chapters 6 and 7. This comparison should answer the question of whether or not selection bias occurred in this study when initially, militias with an Internet presence were selected and those with no presence were excluded from analysis.

Once again, a national group of 28 militias was assembled: 6 militias from the Southeast, 8 from the West, 6 from the Midwest, 2 from the Southwest, and 6 from the East. No claim is made that this list of non-Internet militias is all-inclusive. The point of this comparison is to find a near-matching group of 28 militias to compare with the 28 Internet militias. Table 15 compares the militias by region with those studied earlier in this book. There was no significant difference between the numbers of Internet and non-Internet militias in each of the regions, according to the Chi-Square analysis.

The non-Internet militias selected for study are listed in Table 16. As in Chapter 4, each potential militia to be studied was screened against the operational and conceptual definitions of a militia as constructed in this study. The non-Internet militias qualified sociologically as militias but either (1) had no web site, or (2) did not generate a significant amount of Usenet traffic (defined as 15 or more

**Table 15**
**Internet and Non-Internet Militias by Region**

| Region | Internet | Non-Internet |
|---|---|---|
| Southeast | 7 | 6 |
| West | 9 | 8 |
| Midwest | 7 | 6 |
| Southwest | 3 | 2 |
| East | 2 | 6 |
| Total | 28 | 28 |

Chi-Square = 2.89  with 4 df, p>.50.

total hits in the <u>Deja News</u> archive from 1994-2001). Finally, for the scant Internet data that were available, the data analysis was conducted in the same general manner as for the Internet militias, except that data were not downloaded to diskettes and NUDIST was not used to analyze the data, due to the greatly reduced traffic for these militias. Because of the limited amount of data examined, a formal data analysis was not needed. In addition, because there was very little Internet data available, at times secondary sources outside of the Internet were consulted regarding these militias.

Differences between Groups

The most obvious difference between non-Internet and Internet militias was that the former were not the larger "name" militias that are well known to scholars and to extremist watchers. There were 171 cases in the 28 Internet militias compared with only 31 cases in the 28 non-Internet militias. The non-Internet militias may well be larger than this analysis indicates; however, the 31 cases represent the only cases that could be located, due perhaps to the obscurity of the groups. There is also the distinct possibility that several of the non-Internet militias were among those that went underground or quit in the late 1990s. Finally, the non-Internet militias also are not reported upon extensively in the media. When there are reports, media coverage is local or regional at best.

**Table 16**
**Select Non-Internet Militias by Region**

| | | |
|---|---|---|
| *Southeast* | Alabama Unorganized Militia | Lee County Militia (FL) |
| | Central Arkansas Regional Militia | South Carolina Citizens' Militia |
| | Eastern Diamondbacks (AL) | Tennessee Volunteer Militia |
| *West* | Alameda City Militia (CA) | Unorganized Militia of Arizona |
| | Arizona Patriots | Wyoming Militia |
| | Guardians of American Liberty (CO) | Yakima County Militia (WA) |
| | Oregon Militia | Yavapai County Militia (AZ) |
| *Midwest* | Illinois Minutemen | Western Illinois Militia |
| | Iowa Militia | Wisconsin Free Militia |
| | Southern Kansas Militia | U.S. Militia (MI) |
| *Southwest* | North Texas Militia | Red River Militia (TX) |
| *East* | Hillsborough Co. Dragoons (NH) | Phineas Priesthood (VA) |
| | Maine Militia | Rhode Island Light Infantry |
| | Pennsylvania Militia | Southern Maine Militia |

Comparisons along Smelser's Dimensions

There were no large differences to speak of between the two groups when compared along the dimensions of Smelser's theory. For the most part, the differences discovered were minor and are best viewed as variations upon the general themes that were articulated with respect to the Internet militias. Again, it is important to note that these comparisons are based upon a small number of cases for the non-Internet militias.

The non-Internet groups in general responded to the same kinds of stress as did the Internet groups. A difference between the groups was that the most often mentioned occupation in the non-Internet group was "current or retired military." The Internet group had shown more variety in occupations. However, the same general conclusion can be reached for both groups: there was no evidence of economic marginality based upon the militiaman's occupation.

There was more than one generalized belief found among militiamen in the non-Internet group. This finding parallels what was found among Internet militiamen. One difference discovered was that the non-Internet group was more likely to say that they had been introduced to and accepted the idea of the New World Order prior to joining the militia.

The Branch Davidian conflict at Waco, Texas was the most mentioned precipitant in the non-Internet group and this aligned well with the findings in the Internet group. However, there was generally a more even distribution of responses for all of the precipitants in the non-Internet group. In the Internet group, Waco and Ruby Ridge stood out statistically as the most often mentioned precipitants, accounting for over three fourths of the valid posts relevant to that research question.

The Internet did play an initial role in the formation of several of the militias that are now referred to as "non-Internet." At one time many of these militias had URLs (Web addresses on the Internet) and were linked to and displayed on the web sites of several other militias. However, at some point in time the non-Internet militias pulled their pages off the Web and did not move them to another location. Some of the "bad URLs" were still displayed until relatively recently. For example, as of 2000 there were bad links to the pages of the Lee County Militia and the Regiment of Dragoons, even though their pages have been pulled for some time. We are inclined to believe that these militias either went out of business or went underground.

Tactics did change after the Oklahoma City bombing in that the non-Internet militias tended to drop their pages after the bombing while the Internet group continued for the most part to operate their pages. Posted messages indicate that more secure kinds of communications were engaged in by the non-Internet militiamen, just as in the Internet group. The non-Internet militiamen did not engage in or participate in the rapid growth in Internet traffic due partially to the fact that some militias quit the movement.

For those that carried on for some time after the bombing, it is likely that they did use more secure kinds of communications and not the Internet, according to the messages studied. So the non-Internet group fulfilled the initial research expectations based upon the literature review whereas the Internet group did not. However, despite the fact that the non-Internet groups were probably more likely to go underground, they did not engage in more criminal activity than did the Internet groups, based on the data at hand in Table 17. Finally, as in the Internet group, there was a large proportion of constitutionalists and constitutionalism is the predominant paradigm, based upon the small number of cases examined. In the non-Internet group, however, constitutionalism was the preferred philosophy by more than the approximate 2 to 1 margin that was found in the Internet group.

**Table 17**
**Criminal Involvement of Internet and Non-Internet Militias**

| Crimes Recorded | Internet | Non-Internet | Total |
|---|---|---|---|
| Domestic Terrorism* | 25 | 4 | 29 |
| Militiamen Incarcerated** | 42 | 10 | 52 |
| Total | 67 | 14 | 81 |

Chi Square = .215 with 1 df, p>.50

Notes:      *Cases Prosecuted as of Dec., 1997 (source: Smith and
            Damphousse, 1997).
            **As of Feb. 14, 1998 (source: Pitcavage, 1998).


## Summary

A near-matching group of militias that do not appear on the Internet was studied to see if there were significant differences between those militias and the ones reported on in Chapters 6 and 7. The purpose here was to see if there was a selection bias in our study when we chose to study militias that have an Internet presence.

There were minor differences that could be characterized (for the most part) as variations upon a theme. Non-Internet militia people in general responded to the same kinds of stress as did the Internet militiamen and women. One occupational difference between the groups was noted: the non-Internet militiamen were more likely to report an occupation of "current or retired military." However, the same general conclusion can be reached as in Chapter 6: there was no evidence of economic strain or economic marginality based upon the militiaman's occupation.

There was more than one generalized belief found among militia people in the non-Internet group. This finding parallels what was found among Internet militiamen and women.

Waco was the leading "precipitant" of involvement in the militia movement, as was the case with the Internet militia people.

The non-Internet militiamen and women embraced the Internet, at least initially. As time went on, the non-Internet militias were more likely to drop their web sites, indicating a reduced involvement in the movement, a use of more secure communications, elimination of the group, or "going underground." Thus, the non-Internet militias behaved in a manner more in line with Smelser's theory than did the Internet militias, based upon the limited amount of militias studied. Constitutionalism appeared to be the leading orientation of the non-Internet militias.

# Chapter 9

## Conclusion

In this study, Smelser's theory of collective behavior was selected as the theoretical frame of reference because extant literature about U.S. neo-militias indicated that structural strain and other factors specified by Smelser played a role in the genesis and direction of the movement. In general, this study suggests that Smelser's theory adequately explains the emergence and maintenance of the recent militia movement.

Table 18, summarizing the findings of our study, shows that there is empirical support for Smelser's preliminary point and for four of the five major points. Furthermore, considering that other researchers have confirmed many of the results found here, Smelser's model would appear to have some predictive power. We believe that it may assist social scientists in predicting the next wave of militia activity. Seymour Lipset and Earl Raub (1978) contend that right-wing activity has reappeared at regular intervals throughout U.S. history. Thus, we

**Table 18**
**Summary of Variables, Measurements, and Results**

| *Variable* | *Measured* | *Measurement* | *Comment or Results* |
|---|---|---|---|
| Structural Conduciveness (Preliminary Point) | No | N/A | U.S. social structure conducive to militia development by Constitutional guarantees and by a virtually unregulated forum of communication, the Internet |
| Structural Strain (Major Point 1) | Yes | Militia Web pages, Usenet messages, and interviews | Nine types of strain reported in 125 total messages (Table 5) |
| Generalized Beliefs (Major Point 2) | Yes | Militia Web pages, Usenet messages, and interviews | Three beliefs reported in a total of 110 messages (Table 7) |
| Precipitating Events (Major Point 3) | Yes | Militia Web pages, Usenet messages, and interviews | Ruby Ridge and Waco most reported events in 335 total messages (Table 8) |
| Mobilization for Action (Major Point 4) | Yes | Militia Web pages, Usenet messages, and interviews | Internet preferred medium in a total of 148 messages (Table 9) |
| Social Control (Major Point 5) | Yes | Number of messages posted to Web archive | Social control affects movement but not in direction specified by literature review (Tables 11-12) |
| Ideological Orientation (Variable not part of Smelser's theory) | Yes | Militia Web pages, Usenet messages, and interviews | Constitutionalist messages outnumber Christian Identity by 30% (Table 13) |

have reason to believe that the movement is not currently dead, but in abeyance (Taylor, 1989).

Smelser's model predicts that as long as there is strain, generalized beliefs, precipitating events, and a mobilization for action, there will be another wave of militia activity. We have very little evidence at present that the fears underlying the movement have dissipated or that the generalized beliefs within the movement have lost their power as explanations of the stress being experienced. We do see progress being made in the prevention of precipitating events. Following the Oklahoma City bombing, an unlikely alliance developed between the FBI, selected militias, and academics at Michigan State University (Witkin, 1997). This alliance may have played a role in defusing the Freeman standoff in Montana and several other potential flashpoints. However, Smelser's model also suggests that some permanent structure of dialogue may be necessary to reduce fears and to forestall the possibility of future precipitants. Specifically, a permanent, structured dialogue based on mutual trust (Giddens, 1994) is needed between militiamen and women and the local communities in which they live, and particularly those in positions of authority such as sheriffs, city councils members, community advisory panel members, county boards of supervisors, and others. These locals, untainted by the far-off villains suggested by the generalized beliefs, are in the best position to allow the militias a forum to vent their grievances and to begin to have a modicum of faith restored in contemporary democratic processes.

Where is the militia movement headed? Right now, as it has relocated some of its most serious discussions to a Yahoo! discussion group, it appears to be regrouping and healing some of the bitter, divisive wounds that it suffered in the late 1990s. Within the more restricted environment of the Yahoo group, people who join the group to sow seeds of doubt or to be divisive influences are simply dismissed by the moderator. You can see a certain amount of convalescence going on and we can see that the movement is going back to fundamentals, reviewing the kinds of strains that caused the movement in the first place as well as reinforcing or reiterating the generalized beliefs. Constitutionalism breathes easier and is nurtured in this kind of environment; people advocating for Christian Identity appeared to get bounced, at the discretion of the moderator, a constitutionalist and Internet mentor of the original movement born in 1994.

Only a small proportion, about 19 percent, of the total documents downloaded to disks, were examined in detail for this study. The remainder had no relevance that we could see to Smelser's theory. This suggests that there are ample data that could be used to test alternative theories. For example, how did the neo-militia movement develop relative to the changing opportunity structures and organizational resources available to it? What framing tasks are revealed in the data? The messages could be treated as texts representing the frames used by members to legitimate their cause; this analysis could proceed without having to deal with the issue of the subject's previous or current psychological states, as one must inevitably do with Smelser's theory. In other words, it would not matter if someone who identifies a particular episode as the "precipitating event" for their joining was actually their own precipitant or if they are simply adopting the rhetoric used by other people in their group. More important would be the rhetoric itself and the framing tasks used. As David Snow and Robert Benford (1988) suggest, at least three core framing tasks might be relevant to the militia (and other) movements: (1) diagnosis of some event or aspect of social life as problematic and in need of alteration, (2) a proposed solution to the diagnosed problem that specifies what needs to be done, and (3) a call to arms or rationale for engaging in ameliorative action.

This book has suggested that Internet data can be a viable source of information about militias, so a considerable amount of future militia research on the Internet could advance along the lines of frame analysis, political process, and other models competing with Smelser's.

During the research process it was evident to us that there is an opening to apply at least one theory outside the realm of social movement theory in order to explain what was found in the data. We noted in particular that traditional demographic categories such as gender, region, and social class were not particularly meaningful nor did they shed any light on the findings. Furthermore, there was such variety in the types of militias studied that six general types were developed, along with only a few model or example militias that fit the category well. This meant that the remainder of the militias was made up of hybrids that did not fit well in any category. Thus, sometimes even the variable "orientation" did not prove meaningful, at least when applied at the level of individual militias.

What became distinctively clear after the analysis proceeded were the boundaries being set between individuals in a "camp," of the news group, whether it be Christian Identity, Constitutionalist, Common Law, Posse Comitatus, or anti-militia. Membership in these camps did not depend upon the kinds of demographic or social factors mentioned above, but were more likely to depend upon a very strong common shared language or argot. For instance, case number 83, a well known

Christian Identity militiaman, called his constitutionalist enemies "SMAF's" or Solipcistic Mattoid Anarchy Fascists. Frequent readers of the newsgroup Miscellaneous-Activism-Militia came to accept this as case 83's "put down" of his enemies and after a while this argot becomes familiar to the readers of the newsgroup.

What may be at work here is that militiamen and women in the Internet newsgroups are becoming what sociopolitical ecologist Frederick L. Bates (1997) called a self-referential system. This is a closed system, an organized way of seeing things. As a closed system, the group can adapt to its environment because of shared symbols and language structures. Such adaptation often occurs when changes are made or proposed to the internal operations or internal organization of the system. There was one clear example of this process as work.

After much debate, case 83 was not expelled from the Miscellaneous-Activism-Militia newsgroup in 1999 after he had made several very inflammatory postings. The decision made was that his language was in the tradition of free speech and should not be infringed. His positions were clear and his argot had become more understandable over time. Additionally, the controversy over case 83 prompted discussions about changing the organization of the newsgroup, so that "serious" militia traffic would have its own group, and the related, peripheral traffic would be relocated to another group. The subscribers to M.A.M. thus adapted to case 83's language and mannerisms and continued to operate as a closed system. This could possibly be one of the keys to the longevity of the militia movement as it advances as an Internet phenomenon in abeyance in the new millennium.

Despite the number and quality of worthy alternative theories, we do not at all regret choosing Smelser's theory of collective behavior as the theory to be tested in our research. We continue to believe that Smelser's theory is a powerful explanation for the rise of the neo-militia movement in the United States. It provides a theoretically grounded, logical, and temporal rationale for the appearance of the movement. It is, furthermore, a good match with much of the available secondary source material, and even more important, it is mostly empirically confirmed by the data collected in this study. Only the final component of the theory, social control, was but partially confirmed. Here, social control influenced the movement but not in the specific direction that much of the secondary source material had suggested. Several reasons were given to account for this finding. This is not a reason to reject the theory. In a way, the final component is the least important to Smelser's theory because it occurs after the genesis of the movement.

It was expected that the Internet would provide a valuable data resource for an academic study of militiamen, who are difficult to interview and who are suspicious of academic research. They believe that research data will simply be used as a "control mechanism" by the federal police, or ZOG, or the New World Order to stifle the aims of the movement. It was anticipated that unobtrusive monitoring of Internet traffic would get around the obvious problem of reactivity that might be expected among such a skeptical group of interviewees. In this sense, we believe the research project reported in this book was a success, as we studied a hard to study group and, based upon a limited number of "validating" interviews, appear to have successfully pierced the veil of this most difficult group to understand.

The Internet has already proven its value for those investigating communication processes (e.g. by studying online chat groups), and it may prove to be as valuable to those who are conducting studies aimed at answering substantive sociological research questions such as was the case in this study. Occasionally, though, we were disappointed because the data were not as strong as we would have preferred; this was especially true when seeking private demographic information that was important from the standpoint of research, as in trying to determine a subject's social class. Data on education and income are needed to measure social class adequately, but militiamen and women appeared to be reluctant to reveal this personal information on the Internet, as expected.

Therefore, supplemental face-to-face, phone or e-mail interviews are needed when such information is important to the investigator's research goals. Overall, however, we can conclude that the Internet was a valuable source of information and holds much promise for the future. The question could be raised that if the movement rises again, would it be on the Internet or on a more secure medium? Considering this question, and considering that a more secure medium might be used, it could well be that we have grasped a historic window with which to study and understand the neo-militia movement – one that will perhaps not available in the future.

As noted in Chapter 6, there were many duplicate messages among the militia Internet traffic, and most of it had to do with current events and with issues peripheral to the daily activities of neo-militiamen. There was an effort by some to keep the concept of the New World Order alive by producing (or reproducing) highly conspiratorial evidence that it is still a viable concept. Others appeared to offer up current events as a reminder of sorts what their cause was all about. Taken as a whole, this duplicate traffic would have gotten in the way of the research had it not been for the high speed document reader in the software package QSR-5 (NUDIST). This technological gift rendered moot the issue of duplicate postings as they were basically discovered quickly and deleted from the database.

According to several sources, the number of right-wing extremist organizations in the United States is on the decline. According to the long-time extremist watchers at the Southern Poverty Law Center, the number of citizen militia groups in the U.S. declined from 380 in 1996 to only 73 in 2001. This basically corroborates our analysis as we were able to find a total of 56 militias to study. The Anti-Defamation League also confirms the decline in the number of militia groups after 1996, and also notes the recent deterioration of the three top Ku Klux Klan national groups. ADL additionally reports that the overall number of anti-Semitic incidents is decreasing in recent years -- suggesting, at least, a decline in the number of organized extremist organizations perpetrating these incidents (SPCL, 2003; ADL, 2003; see also CDR, 2003).

Do declining numbers always foretell "the end" of a social movement? Verta Taylor (1989) argued that this is not always the case: many movements go into an "abeyance" mode rather than die out. For example, she notes that the American women's movement did not perish in the 1920s but survived a non-receptive political structure by virtue of its own abeyance structure. Furthermore, as mentioned earlier, Lipset and Raub (1978) in their book on right wing extremism observed how right wing activity has regularly appeared at 15 year intervals throughout American history. This also possibly suggests that the current decline in right wing group membership or activity is only temporary.

The social dynamics of declining movements are not widely studied, unless the movement left a rich legacy of accomplishments or prompted much needed social changes. Obershall's (1978) study of the decline of the leftist social movements of the 1960s appears to be in this spirit. He notes that even though the movements did not succeed in changing the structure of U.S. society, they had an impact by way of pressuring elites and government agencies to commit resources for some goals sought by the movement. With respect to right-wing groups, however, decline is met more often with a sigh of relief from extremist watchers and a concerned public. Attention usually shifts quickly to other, larger threats. Similarly, the attention of academic researchers shifts quickly to "hot" groups -- that is, groups newly formed or discovered, or featured prominently in the news. The dynamics of declining groups is of utmost importance, however, to the long-term survival of the group. How successfully it manages its declining phase may well hold the key to whether the group goes into abeyance so that it can fight another day, or dies out.

An important avenue of future research on militias would look at the movement in decline and how it struggles to maintain membership despite infiltration, organization losses, and declining membership and morale. We have reason to believe at this time that the skillful use of current events is one of many tactics that could play an important role in this process. Over and over, we found that much militia Internet traffic was concerned with current events such as the Clinton impeachment process, the war in Kosovo, the 2000 presidential election, and the 2001 anthrax scare. We believe that current events in general and the numerous controversies generated by them help to refocus militia people on the "frames" that are important to them, help redouble the commitment of the remaining members to the groups' cause, and overall help pump a measure of new life into the organization in spite of its decline. These statements are of course hypotheses, awaiting future study.

# References

Aho, James. 1990. *The Politics of Righteousness: Idaho Christian Patriotism*. Seattle: University of Washington Press.

___. 1994. *This Thing of Darkness: A Sociology of the Enemy*. Seattle: University of Washington Press.

Albers, Benjamin. 2003. "The Militia Movement, Masculinity, and the U.N." Paper presented at the annual meetings of the Southern Sociological Society, New Orleans.

Anti-Defamation League. 1995. *Paranoia as Patriotism: Far-right Influences on the Militia Movement*. New York: Anti-Defamation League.

___. 2003. Anti-Defamation League. <adl.org/adl.asp> (accessed Apr. 15, 2003).

Babbie, Earl. 1995. *The Practice of Social Research*. Belmont: Wadsworth.

Barkun, Michael. 1995. "Militias, Christian Identity and the Radical
    Right." *Christian Century*. 112: 738-740.

___. 1997. *Religion and the Racist Right: The Origins of the Christian
    Identity Movement*. Chapel Hill: University of North Carolina Press.

Bates, Frederick L. 1997. *Sociopolitical Ecology: Human Systems and
    Ecological Fields*. New York: Plenum Press.

Beam, Louis. 1992. "Leaderless Resistance." *Seditionist*. 12: 1-6.

Bell, Daniel. 1963. *The Radical Right*. Garden City: Doubleday.

Bennett, David. 1995. *The Party of Fear: From Nativist Movements to
    the New Right in American History*. New York: Vintage.

Berlet, Chip. 1995a. *Eyes Right! Challenging the Right Wing Backlash*.
    Boston: South End Press.

___. 1995b. "The Violence of Right Wing Populism." *Peace Review*. 7:
    283-288.

___. 2001. "Hard Right Conspiracism and Apocalyptic Millennialism."
    <http://www.publiceye.org/media/hardrit.html>. (accessed Dec. 19,
    2001).

Berlet, Chip and Matthew Lyons. 1995. "Militia Nation." *Progressive*.
    59: 22-25.

___ 2000. *Right Wing Populism in America: Too Close for Comfort*.
    New York: Guilford Press.

Center for Democratic Renewal. 2003. <publiceye.org/cdr/cdr.html>
    (accessed Apr. 15, 2003).

Cheong, Yen. 1995. "Militia chief assails federal stewardship."
    <http://www.yale.edu/ydn/paper/10.27/10.27.95storyno.CE.htm.>
    (accessed Dec. 9, 1999).

*Church and State*. 1995. "Militia Movement Growing in Dozens of
    States, New Reports Indicate." *Church and State*. March: 18-19.

Cockburn, Alexander. 1995. "Beat the Devil." *Nation*. July 17: 80-81.

Corcoran, James. 1991. *Bitter Harvest: Gordon Kahl and the Posse Comitatus*. New York: Viking.

Crothers, Lane. 2002. "The Cultural Foundations of the Modern Militia Movement." *New Political Science*. 24(2) June: 221-234.

*Dallas Morning News*. 1994. "Texas Militias Sound Alarm on Dangers to Freedom." November 28: 18A.

DeArmond, Paul. 1995. "Northwest Beacon: Militia Activity in the Northwest." <http://burn.ucsd.edu/%7Earchive/ats-1/1995.May/0031.html>. (accessed Dec. 9, 1999).

Dees, Morris and James Corcoran. 1997. *Gathering Storm: America's Militia Threat*. New York, NY: Harper Perennial.

Diamond, Sara. 1995. *Roads to Dominion: Right Wing Movements and Political Power in the United States*. New York: Guilford Press.

Dobratz, Betty and Stephanie Shanks-Meile. 1997. *White Power, White Pride! The White Separatist Movement in the United States*. New York: Prentice Hall International.

Donelan, Brenda. 2001. *Extremist Groups of the Midwest: A Content Analysis of Internet Websites*. Dissertation Abstracts International, A: The Humanities and Social Sciences, 61(12) June: 4955-A.

Duffy, James and Alan Brantley. 1998. "Militias: Initiating Contact." <http://fbi.gov/library/leb/1997/July975.htm>. (accessed Aug. 3, 2000).

Flynn, Kevin and Gary Gerhardt. 1995. *The Silent Brotherhood: The Chilling Inside Story of America's Violent Antigovernment Militia Movement*. New York: Signet.

Freilich, Joshua, Jeremy Pienik and Gregory Howard. 2001. "Toward Comparative Studies of the U.S. Militia Movement." *International Journal of Comparative Sociology*. 42(1-2): 163-210.

Gallaher, Carolyn. 2003. *On the Fault Line: Race, Class and the American Patriot Movement*. Lanham: Rowman and Littlefield.

Garner, Roberta and John Tenuto. 1997. *Social Movement Theory and Research: An Annotated Bibliographical Guide*. Lanham: Scarecrow Press.

George, John and Laird Wilcox. 1996. *American Extremists: Militias, Supremacists, Klansmen, Communists, and Others*. Amherst: Prometheus Books.

Giddens, Anthony. 1994. *Beyond Left and Right*. Palo Alto: Stanford University Press.

Halbrook, Stephen. 1984. *That Every Man be Armed: The Evolution of a Constitutional Right*. Albuquerque: University of New Mexico Press.

Halpern, Thomas and Brian Levin. 1996. *The Limits of Dissent: The Constitutional Status of Armed Citizen Militias*. Amherst: Aletheia Press.

Hamilton, Neil. 1996. *Militias in America: A Reference Handbook*. Santa Barbara: ABC-CLIO.

Hamm, Mark. 1996. *Terrorism, Hate Crime and Anti-Government Violence*. Washington, D.C.: National Research Council.

____. 1997. *Apocalypse in Oklahoma: Waco and Ruby Ridge Revenged*. Boston: Northeastern University Press.

Hardy, David. 1985. "The Militia is Not the National Guard." In: M. Norval (ed.), *The Militia in 20th Century America*. (pp. 143-151). Falls Church: Gun Owners Foundation.

Helvarg, David. 1995. "The Anti-Enviro Connection." *Nation*. May 22: 722-724.

Hoffman, Dave. 1995. "America's Militias: Angry White Guys or Defenders of Liberty?" <http://www.webcom.com/haight/features/militia/white.html>. (accessed Dec. 27, 1999).

Hoplight-Tapia, Andrea. 2001. *Subcultural Responses to Y2K.* Dissertation Abstracts International, A: The Humanities and Social Sciences. 61(7) January: 2944-A.

Jones, Harry. 1968. *The Minutemen.* Garden City: Doubleday.

Junas, Dan. 1995. "The Rise of the Militias." <http://caq.com/caq/CAQ.militia.html>. (accessed Dec. 9, 1999).

Kaplan, Jeffrey. 2000. *Encyclopedia of White Power: A Sourcebook on the Radical Racist Right.* Walnut Creek: AltaMira Press.

Kaplan, Jeffrey and Tore Bjorno. 1998. *Nation and Race: The Developing Euro-American Racist Subculture.* Boston: Northeastern University Press.

Kaplan, Jeffrey, and Leonard Weinberg. 1998. *Emergence of a Euro-American Radical Right.* New Brunswick: Rutgers University Press.

Karl, Jonathan. 1995. *The Right to Bear Arms: The Rise of America's New Militias.* New York: Harper Paperbacks.

Kates, Don. 1983. "Handgun Prohibition and the Original Meaning of the Second Amendment." *Michigan Law Review.* 82: 204-273.

Katz, Rebecca and Joey Bailey. 2000. "The Militia, a Legal and Social Movement Analysis: Will the Real Militia Please Stand Up? Militia Hate Group or the Constitutional Militia?" *Sociological Focus.* 33 (2) May: 133-151.

Keen, Carl. 1998. "UF Researcher: Militias are Armed, Dangerous – and Educated." <http://nuance.dhs.org/lbo-talk/9806/0583.html>. (accessed Apr. 13, 2001).

Kemp, Mike. 1998. "Now a Way to Expose Infiltrators."
    <http://www.link2000.net/~preacher/pat4prf1.htm>. (accessed Dec.
    21, 1999).

Kimmel, Michael and Abby Ferber. 2000. "'White Men Are This
    Nation': Right-Wing Militias and the Restoration of Rural
    American Masculinity." *Rural Sociology*. 65(4): 582-604.

Koernke, Mark. 1993. *America in Peril*. Topeka: Prophecy Club.

___. 1994. *Towards the New World Order: America's Secret Police
    Force*. Murray: TRAX.

Kushner, Harvey. 1998. *Terrorism in America: A Structured Approach
    to Understanding the Terrorist Threat*. Springfield: Charles C.
    Thomas.

Lincoln, Yvonne. and Earl Guba. 1985. *Naturalistic Inquiry*. Beverly
    Hills: Sage.

Lindstedt, Martin. 1997. "Second Interview with Militia Members."
    <http://www2.mo-net.com/~mlindste/int72rsp.html>. (accessed
    Feb. 20, 2000).

___. 1998. "Dangerous Liaisons." <http://www2.mo-net.com/
    ~mlindste/mmmisu5.html>. (accessed Dec. 9, 1999).

Lipset, Seymour, and Earl Raub. 1978. *The Politics of Unreason:
    Right-Wing Extremism in America, 1790-1977*. Chicago: University
    of Chicago Press.

Macko, Steve. 1996. "The Aryan Republican Army."
    <http://www.emergency.com/aryanarm.htm>. (accessed Dec. 9,
    1999).

Mason, James. 1997. *Qualitative Researching*. Thousand Oaks: Sage.

McAdam, Doug. 1982. *Political Process and the Development of Black Insurgency, 1930-1970.* Chicago: University of Chicago Press.

McAdam, Doug, John McCarthy, and Meyer Zald. 1988. "Social Movements." In: Neil Smelser. (ed.), *Handbook of Sociology.* (pp. 695-737). London: Sage.

McAlvany, Don. 1990. *Toward a New World Order: The Countdown to Armageddon.* Oklahoma City: Hearthstone.

McFadden, Robert. 1995. "Links in Blast: Armed 'Militia' and a Key Date." *New York Times.* April 22: 1.

Meador, Charlotte. 1996. "Fantasy Theme Chaining in Cyberspace: A Rhetorical Vision of the U.S. Militia Movement." <http://earthops.org/finale.html>. (accessed Dec. 17, 1999).

Merton, Robert. 1938. "Social Structure and Anomie." *American Sociological Review.* 3: 672-682.

Metcalf, Geoff. 1998. "Rumor Control." *World Net Daily.* (December 7).

Miles, Mike, and Alan Huberman. 1994. *Qualitative Data Analysis: An Expanded Sourcebook.* Thousand Oaks: Sage.

Mullins, Wayman. 1993. "Hate Crime and the Far Right: Unconventional Terrorism." In: Kenneth Tunnell (ed.), *Political Crime in Contemporary America* (pp. 121-169). New York: Garland.

Nigel, James. 2001. "Militias, the Patriot Movement, and the Internet: The Ideology of Conspiracism," In: J. Parish and M. Parker (eds.), *The Age of Anxiety: Conspiracy Theory and the Human Sciences* (pp. 63-92). Oxford: Blackwell.

Obershall, Anthony, 1978. "The Decline of the 1960s Social Movements," *Research in Social Movements, Conflicts, and Change.* 1: 257-289.

O'Brien, Sean and Donald Haider-Markel. 1998. "Fueling the Fire:
    Social and Political Correlates of Citizen Militia Activity." *Social
    Sciences Quarterly*. 79: 456-465.

O'Connor, James. 1973. *The Fiscal Crisis of the State*. New York: St.
    Martin's Press.

Parfrey, Adam and Jim Redden. 1994. "Patriot Games." *Village Voice*.
    October 11: 26-31.

Parish, Jane and Martin Parker, 2001. *The Age of Anxiety: Conspiracy
    Theory and the Human Sciences*. Oxford: Blackwell.

Parsons, Talcott and Edward Shils. 1951. *Toward a General Theory of
    Action*. Cambridge: Harvard University Press.

Pierce, William. 1978. *The Turner Diaries*. Washington: National
    Alliance.

Pitcavage, Mark. 1998. "Re: Current Fate of the Minutiae Movement."
    Posted to: Misc-Activism-Militia (accessed Feb. 14, 1998).

____. 2001. "Camouflage and Conspiracy: The Militia Movement from
    Ruby Ridge to Y2K." *American Behavioral Scientist*. 44(6): 957-
    981.

Qualitative Data Solutions (QDS). 1994. *Nonnumerical Unstructured
    Data Indexing Searching and Theorizing*. Melbourne: Qualitative
    Solutions and Research.

Reich, Robert. 2001. *The Future of Success*. London: Heinemann.

Ridgeway, James and Leonard Zeskind. 1995. "Revolution USA."
    *Village Voice*. May 2: 23-26.

Robertson, Pat. 1991. *The New World Order*. Dallas: Word Publishing.

Salsich, Peter. 1961. "The Armed Superpatriots in the Midwest."
    *Nation*. November 11: 372-274.

Schneider, Keith. 1994. "Fearing a Conspiracy, Some Heed a Call to Arms." *New York Times*. November 14: 1.

Sherwood, Samuel. 1994. *Establishing an Independent Militia in the United States*. Blackfoot: Founder's Press.

Skocpol, Theda and John Campbell. 1995. *American Society and Politics: Institutional, Historical, and Theoretical Perspectives*. New York: McGraw-Hill.

Smelser, Neil. 1963. *Theory of Collective Behavior*. New York: Free Press of Glencoe.

Smith, Brent. 1994. *Terrorism in America: Pipe Bombs and Pipe Dreams*. Albany: State University of New York Press.

Smith, Brent and Kelly Damphousse. 1998. "Preliminary Results from the American Terrorism Study: Characteristics of Groups and Persons Indicted under the FBI's Counterterrorism Program, 1990-1997." Paper Presented at the Annual Meetings of the American Society of Criminology, Washington, D.C.

Snow, David and Leon Anderson. 1993. *Down on Their Luck: A Study of Homeless Street People*. Berkeley: University of California Press.

Snow, David and Robert Benford. 1988. "Ideology, Frame Resonance, and Participant Mobilization." *International Social Movement Research*. 1: 197-217.

Snow, David, E. Burke Rochford, Steven Worden and Robert Benford. 1986. "Frame Alignment Processes, Micromobilization, and Movement Participation." *American Sociological Review*. 51: 464-481.

Snow, Robert. 1999. *The Militia Threat: Terrorists Among Us*. New York: Plenum.

Southern Poverty Law Center (SPLC). 1996. *False Patriots: The Threat of Anti-Government Extremists*. Montgomery: SPLC.

___. 1997. *Active Patriot Groups in the U.S. in 1996*. Montgomery: SPLC.

___. 1998. *Active Patriot Groups in the U.S. in 1997*. Montgomery: SPLC.

___. 2003. SPLC Main Page. <http://www.splcenter.org>. (accessed Apr. 15, 2003.

State of California. 1965. *Paramilitary Organizations in California*. Sacramento: Office of the Attorney General.

Stern, Kenneth. 1995. *Militias, a Growing Danger*. New York: American Jewish Committee.

___. 1996. *A Force Upon the Plain*. New York: Simon and Schuster.

Swomley, Jon. 1995. "Armed and Dangerous; the Threat of the 'Patriot Militias.'" *Humanist*. 55: 8-11.

Taylor, Verta. 1989. "Social Movement Continuity: The Women's Movement in Abeyance." *American Sociological Review*. 54: 761-775.

Texas Militia Papers (TMP). 1996. <http://constitution.org/mil/tmp.htm>. (accessed Jul. 15, 2000).

Thompson, Linda. 1993. *Waco, the Big Lie*. Indianapolis: American Justice Federation.

___. 1994. *Waco II, the Big Lie Continues*. Indianapolis: American Justice Federation.

Turner, Billy. 2001. "Domestic Terrorism." In: *Encyclopedia of Criminology and Deviant Behavior: Millennium Issue, Vol. 2* (pp. 498-501). London: Francis and Taylor.

U.S. Bureau of the Census. 1994. *Statistical Abstract of the United States*.   Washington: USGPO.

U.S. Senate. 1982. *The Right to Keep and Bear Arms. Subcommittee on the Constitution of the Committee on the Judiciary, 97th Congress, 2nd Session*. Washington: USGPO.

____. 1997. *The Militia Movement in the United States: Hearings Before the Subcommittee on Terrorism, Technology and Government Information of the Committee on the Judiciary*. Washington: GPO.

Van Dyke, Nella and Sarah Soule. 2002. "Structural Social Change and the Mobilizing Effect of Threat: Explaining Levels of Patriot and Militia Organizing in the United States." *Social Problems*. 49(4): 497-520.

Walker, Sam. 1994. "'Militias' Forming Across U.S. to Protest Gun Control Laws." *Christian Science Monitor*. October 17: 1.

Walter, Jess. 1995. *Every Knee Shall Bow: The Truth and Tragedy of Ruby Ridge and the Weaver Family*. New York: Harper Paperbacks.

Weber, Max. 1947. *The Theory of Social and Economic Organization*. Glencoe: The Free Press.

Weeber, Stan C. 1999. "Origins, Orientations and Etiologies of the U.S. Citizen Militia Movement, 1982-1997." *Free Inquiry in Creative Sociology*. 27(1): 57-66.

____. 2001. *Internet and U.S. Citizen Militias*. Denton: University of North Texas Libraries.

Weinberg, Leonard. 1993. "The American Radical Right: Exit, Voice and Violence." In: P. Merkl and L. Weinberg (eds.), *Encounters With the Contemporary Radical Right* (pp. 185-203). Boulder: Westview Press.

Whitley, John. 1998. "New World Order Intelligence Update." <http://Home.InfoRamp.Net/~jwhitley>. (accessed Aug. 21, 1998).

Williams, David. 1991. "Civic Republicanism and the Citizen Militia: the Terrifying Second Amendment." *Yale Law Journal*. 101: 551-615.

Wills, Garry. 1995. "The New Revolutionaries." *New York Review of Books*. August 10: 50-55.

Witkin, Gordon. 1997. "The Secret FBI-Militia Alliance." *U.S. News and World Report*. May 12: 40-41.

# Appendices

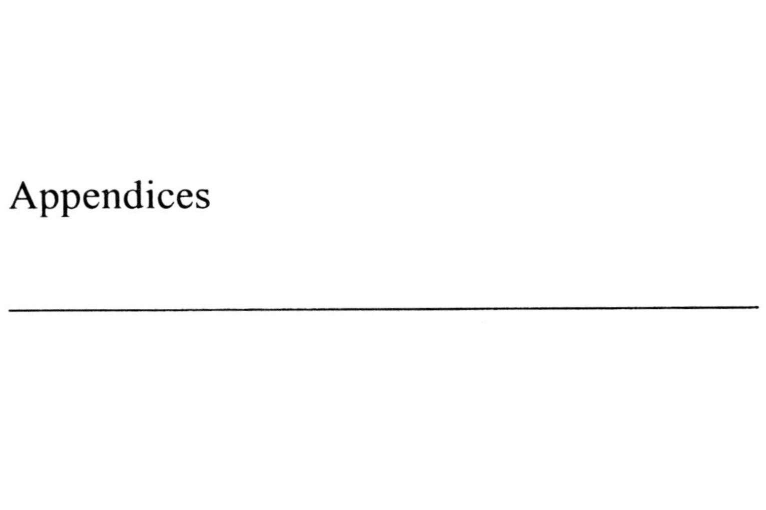

# Appendix A:
# A Note about USENET

---

Usenet is a discussion system that is distributed world-wide. It consists of a set of news groups with names that are classified by subject. Messages are "posted" to these newsgroups by people on computers with the appropriate software. This software must be offered by the computer owner's Internet service provider. Just because a computer user has Internet access does not automatically mean that the user has access to Usenet.

Some newsgroups are moderated. In these newsgroups, the messages are first sent to a moderator before appearing in the newsgroup. The three newsgroups studied here were all moderated, so that messages with extreme sexual content, or ones that were determined to be otherwise offensive to a broad general audience, were not published in the newsgroup. However, beyond that, all views were permitted on a "free speech" basis.

Usenet is not the same as the Internet. The Internet is a wide-ranging network, parts of which are subsidized by various governments. The Internet carries many kinds of traffic (including e-mail) of which Usenet is only one kind. Furthermore, the Internet is only one of the various networks that carry Usenet traffic.

Usenet is also not a "UUCP" network. UUCP is a protocol for sending data over point-to-point connections, typically using dial up modems. Sites use UUCP to carry many kinds of traffic, of which Usenet is only one. UUCP, furthermore, is only one of the various transports carrying Usenet traffic.

# Appendix B: Research Questions, Key Concepts, and Keywords for NUDIST Data Searches

---

**APPENDIX B**
**RESEARCH QUESTIONS, KEY CONCEPTS AND KEYWORDS**
**FOR NUDIST DATA SEARCHES**

| Question 1: | Did militiamen/women experience strain prior to or during their tenure in the militia? | | | |
|---|---|---|---|---|
| *Key* *Concept:* | Strain | | | |
| *Keywords:* | Change | Displaced | Illegitimate | Prestige |
| | Children | Divorce | Illness | Socialism |
| | Collectivism | Downhill | Income | Soviet |
| | Communism | Downward | Layoff | Status |
| | Control | Mobility | Living | Strain |
| | Corrupt | Fear | Occupation | Work |

**APPENDIX B, continued**
**RESEARCH QUESTIONS, KEY CONCEPTS AND KEYWORDS**
**FOR NUDIST DATA SEARCHES**

| Question 2: | Before joining the militia, or during militia membership, were militiamen/women introduced to the idea of the New World Order, and did they accept it? | | | |
|---|---|---|---|---|
| *Key Concept:* | New World Order | | | |
| *Keywords:* | Bilderbergers<br>Black<br> helicopters<br>Federal<br> Reserve<br>FEMA | Gurkha<br> troops<br>Illuminati<br>Masonic<br>New World<br> Order | NWO<br>Occupying<br> troops<br>Regionalism<br>Rockefeller<br>Rothschild | Russian<br> troops<br>Trilateralists<br>Zionists |

| Question 3: | Were events at Ruby Ridge and Waco, together with the passage of gun control legislation, important reasons why participants joined the militia? | | | |
|---|---|---|---|---|
| *Key Concept:* | Precipitant | | | |
| *Keywords:* | Anti-Brady<br>ATF<br>Autonomy<br>Brady Bill<br>Brady II | Bureaucracy<br>Estes Park<br>Gun control<br>Koresh<br>LA Riot | MOVE<br>Pratt<br>Roland<br>Ruby Ridge | Violent<br> crime act<br>Waco<br>Weaver |

| Question 4: | Did the Internet play a more important role than other media (i.e., short-wave radio, e-mail, and fax) in helping to mobilize the movement? | | | |
|---|---|---|---|---|
| *Key Concepts:* | Internet | Alternative media | | |
| *Keywords:* | BBS<br>Bulletin<br> board | Computer<br>E-mail<br>Fax | Internet<br>Short-wave<br> radio | Usenet |

## APPENDIX B, continued
## RESEARCH QUESTIONS, KEY CONCEPTS AND KEYWORDS
## FOR NUDIST DATA SEARCHES

| | | | |
|---|---|---|---|
| **Question 5:** | Following the Oklahoma City bombing, did social control influence movement participants to use the Internet less and "underground" kinds of communication more often? | | |
| *Key Concept:* | Mode of communication | | |
| *Keywords:* | ARA | Cut-out | McVeigh | Strausmeier |
| | Brescia | John Doe | Nichols | Tactics |
| | Cell | John Doe II | Resistance | Tri-States |
| | Centennial Park | Leaderless | Security | Underground |

| | | | |
|---|---|---|---|
| **Question 6:** | What is the primary ideological orientation of the movement, constitutionalist or Christian Identity? | | |
| *Key Concepts:* | Christian Identity | | Constitutional Republic |
| *Keywords:* | Apocalypse | Colonial | Oklahoma City | Socialism |
| | Aryan | Constitution | | Taxation |
| | Christian | Covenant | Republic | Yahweh |
| | Collectivism | Identity | Sheeple | |

# Appendix C: Data Gathering Procedures

As mentioned in Chapter 4, information from web pages and from Usenet was downloaded to diskettes for analysis. After the downloaded information was converted to Microsoft Word files, NUDIST was used to analyze the data.

NUDIST is a software program that was designed to look for keyword and chunks of text that pertain to the research questions. These keywords appear in Appendix B.

NUDIST searches for the relevant keyword and then generates a report. The report lists the files in which the keyword appears along with a printout of the data chunk (the sentences immediately prior to and following the appearance of the keyword.)

There were 94 keywords relevant to the research questions, and therefore 94 reports were generated that were subsequently reviewed.

In reviewing the reports, each chunk that appeared to have substance to answer a research question was noted and the original file was found on the disk. The hard copy of the file was the raw data from which a number of coding decisions could be made (see Appendix E for detailed coding instructions).

Some keywords were added or deleted based upon what was in the reports. This was expected because in qualitative research, codes often have to be added, reconstituted or deleted as the analysis proceeds (Lincoln and Guba, 1985; Snow and Anderson, 1993; Miles and Huberman, 1994; Mason, 1997).

In summary, the basic steps in the data collection process were these:

- locate most important files on disks, based on the NUDIST reports
- produce hard copy of the document
- examine document for manifest and latent content
- code according to instructions, making note of codes that need to be added, combined, or deleted

# Appendix D: Coding of Militiamen and Women's Occupations

Occupations were coded according to U.S. Census Bureau (1994) categories as follows:

Professional/managerial

Executive, administrative and managerial personnel and those with professional specialties (including business owners and current and retired military).

Sales, Technical

Technicians and related support; sales occupations; administrative support, including clerical (including reports of middle class standing with no elaboration; and reports of government work with no elaboration).

Manual labor

Precision production and crafts; repair work; operators, fabricators, and laborers (including reports of lower middle class or working class with no elaboration).

Service, Low Skill

Service occupations, farming, forestry, and fishing.

# Appendix E: Coding Instructions for Research Questions

The reports generated by NUDIST indicated the files that might have relevance to each of the research questions. Each file was then checked and each document that helped to answer any of the research questions was examined for its manifest and latent content. (A complete description of this process appears in Appendix C, Data Gathering Procedures). The paragraphs below describe how the variables were operationalized and how specific messages were coded. The variables coded are those suggested by the research questions, i.e., structural strain, generalized belief, precipitant, mobilization for action, social control, and ideological orientation.

## Structural Strain

Smelser (1963) argues that structural strain is a precondition for the development of a social movement. He delineates four different types of strain that he believes is most common as preconditions for a social movement; however, he concedes that any kind of strain can produce any kind of collective behavior, including social movements.

Consequently, in this study the decision was made not to exclude any kinds of strains that might be reported by the militiamen. Additionally, particular attention was paid to the militiaman or woman's occupations as some of the literature suggested that downward occupational mobility is an important strain that may have preceded the appearance of the neo-militia movement.

Nine kinds of strain emerged from the content analysis of the web pages and Usenet messages. These strains were coded as follows: (1) fear of federal and/or international police forces; (2) fear of federal government (general); (3) fear that the U.S. is becoming more like the former Soviet Union; (4) rapid social change; (5) distrust of government and/or discontent with government; (6) economic distress or stress (general); (7) shrinking or declining standard of living; (8) globalization and/or loss of jobs; and (9) other strains not classifiable.

Militiamen and women's occupations, as revealed in Internet messages, were coded according to U.S. Census Bureau (1994) categories as follows: (1) professional and managerial; (2) sales/technical; (3) manual labor; and (4) service and low skill. See Appendix D for a full description of the occupations coded in each of these four categories.


Generalized Beliefs


To Smelser (1963), strain alone was not sufficient for a social movement to appear. It must be accompanied by at least one generalized belief that put the participant's stress into a context and gives an explanation for the kinds of stress being experienced. Messages whose manifest or latent content indicated that the militiaman had heard of the New World Order and accepted the concept as a frame of reference for explaining their stresses prior to joining the militia, or during militia membership, were coded 1. This includes explicit remarks by individuals indicating acceptance of the NWO prior to joining the militia, or during militia membership, and support as inferred from individual remarks or group statements (declarations). In all cases it must be surmised or inferred from the messages that this support occurred prior to joining the militia or during militia membership.

A code of 2 was assigned those messages that indicated the militiaman had not heard of the New World Order, or if having been introduced to the concept prior to joining the militia, or during militia membership, did not believe in or accept the idea as a frame of reference for understanding the kinds of stresses they had been experiencing. This includes explicit remarks that the NWO is not important or that other concepts are more important, or the same result as inferred implicitly from remarks posted.


Precipitating Events


According to Smelser (1963), the existing strains accompanied by generalized beliefs are not enough to produce an episode of collective behavior; in his value-added theory he specified that precipitating events are crucial. These events confirm the explanations for stress generated by the generalized belief and crystallize calls for action. In this study, there were seven coding categories for precipitants. The categories, and the code assigned, are as follows: Waco (coded 1); Ruby Ridge (coded 2); Brady Bill (coded 3); Assault Weapons Bill of 1994 (coded 4); 1992 Estes Park Meeting (coded 5); President George Bush's New World Order Speech of 1991 (coded 6); and the L.A. Riot of 1992 or the MOVE bombing or Desert Storm (coded 7). Militiamen/women could mention more than one precipitant in a given message.


Mobilization for Action


Given the appearance of strain, generalized beliefs, and precipitating events, there is still a possibility that no social movement will emerge, unless there is a mobilization for action in which certain key individuals take the lead (Smelser, 1963). Because it has been suggested that the Internet provided a platform for leaders to move quickly to mobilize the movement, the variable, "mobilization for action," was concerned with the type of media that the militiamen believed were most helpful in mobilizing the movement. These media were coded as follows: bulletin boards or Usenet or Internet (coded 1); FAX (coded 2); short-wave radio (coded 3); talk shows, cable TV or videos (coded 4); e-mail (coded 5) and direct mail (coded 6).

Militiamen or women could report more than one favorite media in any given message.

Social Control

Social control in Smelser's (1963) terms referred to the mechanisms that affected the direction of a movement once it had begun. It is the sum total of mechanisms that disrupt or inhibit a movement in progress (and not social control in the sense of enforcing norms.) In this study we are primarily concerned with the electronic implications of the Oklahoma City bombing and specifically, from an electronic standpoint, if Internet traffic was abandoned for more secure kinds of communications such as encrypted e-mail messages or the confidential communications within small leaderless cells. This variable was measured by traffic as recorded in the Usenet archive <u>Deja News</u>.

<u>Deja News</u> is the repository of messages posted to the Usenet groups that in turn became the raw data of this study. A specialty feature of this archive is the <u>Deja News</u> Power Search function that allows researchers to search for messages by author, by date of posting, and by newsgroup. Using Power Search, a researcher can determine how many messages have been posted to miscellaneous-activism-militia, talk-politics-guns and miscellaneous-survivalism for two time frames (two different periods of time) after the Oklahoma City bombing. For talk-politics-guns and miscellaneous-survivalism, it is necessary to use the screening word "militia" in the Power Search in order to count those messages that had specific content relevant to militias. Both of these groups have many discussions that are only peripherally related to militias (e.g., second amendment and survivalism issues), so use of the screening word helped to screen out this mostly irrelevant discussion. Unfortunately, <u>Deja News</u> was discontinued in 2001. After that, the exact kinds of measurements we were looking for were not available.

The two time frames were selected in order to grasp the long term trends in militia traffic after the Oklahoma City bombing. The first time frame is 1-20 months after the bombing and the second is 21-40 months after the bombing.

## Ideological Orientation

Left unresolved by the literature review was the issue of the ideological orientation of the neo-militia movement. There was a difference of opinion among writers who stressed the constitutionalism of the militias and those who believed that Christian Identity beliefs underlay most all of the militia rhetoric. Therefore, in this study the variable "orientation" was concerned with whether the primary ideology of the militia was constitutionalist or Christian Identity.

Messages of which manifest or latent content indicated that the purpose of the militia is to restore a Constitutional Republic, or were otherwise supportive of the constellation of beliefs known as constitutionalism, were coded 1. Messages whose manifest or latent content was supportive of Christian Identity goals were coded 2. The following are examples of messages coded 1:

> Once we got past the race card and people understood that we were not any of the things that certain areas of the media were saying – because we have Jewish commanders; we have black commanders; ... joining us, and we're trying to make a positive force here in Michigan to change our government back to the Constitution (post 25).

> Purposes (of the Georgia Militia)... to execute the Laws of the Union, suppress Insurrections, and repel Invasions (post 30).

> ...the bulk of the...militias of the various United States have formed a grass-root response to such government-sponsored terrorism as well as the continued degradation of our Constitutional rights at the hands of the current federal administration (post 31).

The following are examples of messages coded 2:

> Other elements that occurred since the high-water mark for the open Constitutional militia movement... have strengthened my conclusion that the CI (Christian Identity) and White Nationalist Resistance cells have their place in our Patriot coalition... (post 51).

> Thomas (ARA leader) said he met Guthrie, nicknamed "Wild Bill", at Aryan Nations headquarters in 1991 (post 70).

> Frankly... you hate White People. You really hate those of us who are fighting to restore White America for White People. I point out that if you hate us so much, you simply have no right to live as a parasite off of us and among us. We neither want nor need to have you around. Go live among those you serve. Practice what you preach (post 78).

# Index

C



D



E



F